HOW TO BECOME AN INDEPENDENT SYSTEMS THINKER:

TURN OFF AUTOPILOT AND LEARN TO THINK FAST, MAKE THE BEST DECISIONS OF YOUR LIFE, THROUGH AN EFFECTIVE STEP-BY-STEP THINKING MODEL;

DECLUTTER   YOUR MIND AND SOLVE COPLEX PROBLEMS

Ray Crystal

Table Of Content

Introduction

Systems that think as they do in modern times have been around for approximately 60 years but have only had a relatively large audience among non-scientists within the last decade. Thinking structures is a way to look at things, individuals, and organizations worldwide. It consists of principles and methods that give system-thinkers a new, potentially expanding worldview rather than a series of static methodologies or theories.

Systems that think, also called systems thinking, is a school of thought drawn from multiple disciplines, including systems theory in the natural and social sciences, research on human knowledge representation, linguistics, philosophy, psychology, cognitive science, management science, architecture, and organizational design, cybernetics, computers, and software development. Thinking structures encourages observation-based, practical, and creative thinking, instead of that which is inferred from theories, formulas, rules, or Logic.

Here are the four principles that form the essence of thinking structures:

1. Thinking structures are sets of principles and methods that together give system-thinkers a new, potentially expanding worldview.

2. Not all systems thinking is the same. Systems represent things, activities, and properties. Systems exist at different levels. How these systems are interconnected differ? To be effective, systems thinking must be sensitive to the different ways in which these systems interconnect.

3. Thinking structures are an alternative to thinking methods, which, as methods, prescribe instead of providing principles and methods for thinking about individuality, organizations, and society.

4. Thinking methods are constants. Thinking structures are metaphors.

In some way, structures don't exist objectively and rely on the human observer to see entities or processes as structures. However, it can be beneficial to consider events in the world as structures and make sense of their behavior. Thinkers of structures prefer to consider the environment as a series of ongoing interactions, changes, and processes. Systems analysis, in a way, complements the instrumental view offered by mainstream reductionist science.

Thinking structures are by no means a limited set of rules or formulas. They offer ways of seeing experience in new and provocative ways. Systems thinking about any particular event can lead to unexpected conclusions. Such negative results are typical in science. To overcome them, however, theories are always built on a reliable foundation of knowledge. Neither reductionist science nor systems thinking rely on formulas. There are three significant differences between them.

First, reductionist science is a way of representing reality in a formulaic form. Systems thinking is by no means a straitjacket.

Second, systems thinking is not just a hypothesis about the world that is validated by evidence. It is an alternative to thinking scientifically.

Third, science sees entities as static, isolated, and independent. However, systems-thinkers see entities as structures in a context and acknowledge that their behavior is to an unknown extent variable and mostly unpredictable. Thoughts about structures are always changeable and reliant on interpretations - even after centuries, new facts and evidence can cause old theories to be replaced.

Throughout the book, we will look at various archetypes of typical ways in which systems function, and more importantly, how they become dysfunctional over time if we don't examine how the dynamic works. This allows us to look beyond mere events to the patterns of behavior within the system itself that lead up to them. It's a powerful mechanism wherein we become active instead of reactive to events as they occur. Understanding the dynamic can be a very constructive way of leading us to a new behavioral and cognitive ability to assess circumstances from the systems point of view instead of a systematic approach to problem-solving.

Chapter 1: Essential Thinking Skills

Tools for Systems Thinkers

Interconnectedness

From linear to circular, systems thinking demands a change in mindset.

The shift's principle is that everything is connected. We discuss interconnectedness not in a manner but a biological sciences manner. Everything depends upon something else for survival. Humans and trees need air, food, and sunlight, and carbon dioxide, respectively, to flourish. Everything requires something different, an intricate collection of things, to endure. Inanimate objects will also be reliant on different things: a seat desires a tree to supply its timber to expand, and a mobile phone requires electricity supply. So, once we say 'what's interconnected' out of a system thinking perspective, we're defining a basic existence principle. From this, we could alter how we view the planet from a linear, ordered" mechanical worldview' into a lively, chaotic, interconnected variety of connections and feedback loops. A systems thinker employs this mentality to operate and to entangle inside the complexity of life.

Synthesis

Synthesis refers to make something fresh. The aim is synthesis, instead of analysis into manageable parts, when it comes to systems thinking. Analysis matches into the reductionist and mechanical worldview. However, all programs are dynamic and frequently complex; hence, we need a more holistic understanding. Synthesis is all about knowing the elements and the whole at precisely the same time, in addition to the relationships. Synthesis has the capacity.

Emergence

From a systems standpoint, we all know that bigger things emerge from components: development is the consequence. In the abstract sense, development refers to the universal idea of how life stems from different biological components in varied and unique ways. Emergence is the result of these components' synergies; it's all about nonlinearity and self-organization, and we frequently use the term' development' to characterize the results of things socializing together. A straightforward case of development is a snowflake. It creates components and ecological variables. After the temperature is correct, freezing water particles form in unique fractal patterns around one molecule of thing, including a speck of contamination, a spore, or perhaps dead skin cells. Conceptually, we frequently find development somewhat tricky to get our mind around. Still, once we get it, our mind begins to form emergent results from the different and frequently strange things you experience in th8e entire world.

Feedback Loops

Since everything is connected, you will find flows and feedback loops between components of a system. When we know dynamics and their kind, we can detect, comprehend, and detract from feedback loops. The two forms of feedback loops are balancing, and both are reinforcing. What may be confusing is that a feedback loop is not a fantastic thing. This occurs when components in a system fortify more like algae growing exponentially in a pond or population growth. A wealth of a single component can refine in strengthening loops. A balancing feedback loop is where things balance out. Nature nearly got this down to a tee with a predator/prey scenario – however, if you take out a lot of a single creature in an ecosystem, the next thing you know, you have a population explosion of a different, that's the other sort of opinions -- strengthening.

Causality

Understanding feedback loops are all about gaining a standpoint of causality: how something contributes to a different thing in a dynamic and continuously evolving platform (all methods are dynamic and always changing somehow; that's the heart of life). Cause and effect are all reasonably common theories in several professions and life generally -- parents attempt to teach this kind of crucial life lesson to their young ones, and I am confident that you can recall a recent time you're at the forefront of an effect in an unintentional activity. As a theory in systems thinking, causality is about decoding how things affect each other in a method. Understanding contributes to a perspective on service, feedback connections loops, and relationships, which are parts of systems mapping.

Systems Mapping

Systems mapping is among the tools of these systems thinkers. There are several approaches to map, from bunch mapping to complex feedback evaluation. On the other hand, principles and the principles of all systems mapping are worldwide. Identify and map the components of things' inside a method to comprehend how they interconnect, link, and behave in an intricate system, and out of here, unique discoveries and insights may be used to create interventions, changes, or coverage decisions that will radically alter the machine in the best way. His introduction into six essential concepts is a crucial building block for creating a more detailed view of how the world functions from a systems standpoint and will improve your ability to think divergently and creatively to get a favorable effect.

Guidelines for Daily Systems Thinking Practice

Individual Practice

Becoming a system thinker begins with a powerful Commitment to creating abilities and awareness.

Ask Unique Question

Systems thinking provide a frame for solving problems in addition to defining issues. To practice thinking out of a systemic standpoint, begin that you ask. Try to ask questions that get at underlying structural connections or patterns of behavior exhibited over time, which concentrate your attention on possible flaws, strengthening or balancing procedures, and unintended consequences, which help you comprehend what periods you are focusing on and how you and others are controlling scenarios.

Learn to Experience Time Differently

When confronted with issues, we're strongly influenced by the messages of society about what constitutes time. We concentrate on periods that are shorter than we should.

To fight this, consider that which you're currently working, making the period horizon

By way of instance, are you currently interested in oil prices' behavior since they go over an interval or a span? What could be a suitable time horizon for realizing the effect of disposal?

Additionally, extend your awareness of exactly what constitutes "the present."

Try thinking concerning a block of time as "currently"--say, one year ago and one year. Ask yourself exactly what happened. What's happening? What does the next year hold? By extending our awareness of "today," we could grasp interconnections we might not have seen previously.

Notice the Systems around You

Consider searching for feedback loops in typical scenarios. By way of instance, has your business started a new product whose sales took off to plateau out? This may suggest a process that is influenced by using a procedure. Are you attracted like a yo-yo involving two extremes? If this is so, a loop is on the job.

Keep an eye on the effect your actions have in cycles or your family system

Might there be a loop broken if you choose your socks up? If the – tap is turned off while brushing your teeth, what might happen?

Bring a Loop-a-Day (or just per week). Each morning sits down with your cup of coffee, the paper, a pad of paper, and a pencil, and search for news stories which you could research through causal loop diagrams. Look. (By way of instance, "The unemployment rate climbed over the previous ten decades, as did the number of households looking for welfare support.") Sketch the arrangement which you believe is currently creating these routines. This is a superb way to practice controlling loop diagramming and understanding structures that are systemic. The Economist magazine is a prosperous source of systems-oriented stories.

Ray Crystal

Chapter 2: Mental Models

At their most basic level, mental models explain the thought process one has regarding the way things in the real-world work. The relationship between the various parts of what is being analyzed and one's actions, feelings, consequences, etc., are taken into account to interpret potential consequences, outcomes, and more.

This is mostly a very detailed breakdown of a process that occurs quite organically and seemingly involuntarily. To keep track of mental models, analyze them, and change them is a fundamental part of mastering your mental fortitude and eliminating the barriers that stand between you and what you want in life. When you think about what keeps you from achieving the things you want in life, you will generally find that some combination of your mindset and external circumstances prevented success.

Knowing this, we take another step to unravel that mental process. The more factors we can take control of a situation, the more likely it is to emerge successfully. That makes a fair bit of sense, doesn't it? That's the aim of this writing and the information in it.

What is Mental Model?

A mental model, simply put, is a representation of the simple mechanics of something. This is a comprehensive statement, but mental models are inherently broad, as you can apply a model to anything in life. We can't keep every minute detail of everything we encounter globally, so these models simplify the more complex aspects of life into more digestible and organizable units.

What are these mental models of which I speak? I'm glad you asked because mental models are the foundation of your entire reality. Understanding them is critical to understanding yourself and your life.

Most people take reality at face value. They assume that life is as they see it. But the reality of reality is that it is subjective, based on each person's unique perception and imagination. A lot of factors go into shaping one's reality. The result is that no two people see anything the same way.

This leads to a lot of conflict in the world, but it can also lead to poor decisions based on a limited understanding of reality. Mental models are what you use to read reality, and a problematic one can undoubtedly make your life more challenging because it prevents you from seeing reality with clarity.

A mental model is a representation of the human mind's thought process. Mental models are how we understand the world. Not only do they shape what we think and how we understand situations, but they drive our decisions and feelings. They lay the fundamental basis for our lives. What makes mental models tricky is that they are not just influenced by reality – but instead, they draw from a series of experiences, biases, and even a person's current mood. Shaped by culture, personal experiences, and background, they are as unalike as snowflakes from person to person. Two children raised in the same household will have two very different mental models, despite having similar backgrounds and the same culture.

Everything that a person sees, hears, and otherwise senses are represented by mental models inside their minds. Mental models are used as scales by which a person automates decisions and internalizes external stimuli. As mentioned by scientists, the Internal scales are ever-changing and unstable as the human mind is susceptible to change due to adaptation. They are also variable since every person has a different outlook and thus a different set of models.

Mental models use perception to drive reasoning and decisions. This reasoning can be flawed at times. Every bit of reasoning you engage in is driven by your perception, no matter how erroneous it may be, as well as dozens or even hundreds of other factors that you may not be aware of.

For example, you may avoid spending time with someone who has a lot of tattoos because you were raised to believe that people with tattoos are lowlifes, but you are not aware of that bias, and you simply dislike someone based on his body modifications. Meanwhile, another person would not have that bias because he was raised differently, so he has no problem hanging out with heavily tattooed people. Your mental model drives you to decide on a person you may not even be consciously aware of.

Furthermore, mental models drive priorities. One woman may consider getting her hair and nails done every few weeks an utmost priority, while another woman does not consider those things necessary at all. Your mental model helps you rate things based on importance so that you can dedicate time, money, and energy to something that you consider worthwhile. Not everyone will agree with your priorities because everyone has a different rating system for importance in life.

Mental models are imperfect because they lack complete information. You can't know everything and focus on everything in the world. You can only focus on a few tiny parts that fit into your accepted reality. Therefore, your lens of reality is relatively narrow, yet it shapes many decisions that can be quite huge.

Think about this example: You support a particular political healthcare proposal because you recognize a few problems, probably problems that affect you personally somehow, with the current system. Your vote this way. However, other people disagree with your accepted healthcare model because they see different problems with the model that you cannot see from your perspective. Thus, you don't understand why people disagree with you, and you feel frustrated.

Your mind will create a small-scale model with the evidence it currently possesses for each situation it encounters. This model will include predicted outcomes of each situation and each decision. Whether or not these outcomes are accurate is hard to say. Sometimes you are right; frequently, you are wrong.

Mental models are paradoxical. Some are quite fluid and change with time and experience. That is why you are a different person now than you were ten years ago, twenty years ago, and so on. You begin to change mental models throughout your life and adapt them to fit what you need. Yet, mental models are also incredibly rigid. Some stay with you for life. Others may be fluid, but your mind relies on them so heavily that it applies them to every area of life, even areas of life that don't benefit from the said mental model.

The takeaway here is that mental models can be changed and adapted to become more helpful. However, you must work hard on your mind to undo years of experience that has created the models. You must also perform some brutally honest introspection to uncover the real roots of specific thoughts and actions that you routinely engage in. You must be able to let your ego down for a second and say, "Hey, I'm not doing something right. I need to make a change."

Why is this mental work worthwhile? The fact is that your reasoning is not based on logic or rules but rather on mental models. So, if you are operated on a flawed mental model, you are depriving yourself of the ability to use logic to arrive at the ideal decision. Your decisions are influenced in a direction that may not be beneficial in the long run, even though you think they are significant decisions. Learning to recognize mental models and focus on Logic instead can help you make the best decisions for yourself.

Also, since mental models vary from person to person, what works for you may not work for anyone else. This is why your decisions can create a lot of negative conflict within your family, relationship, or team at work. Learning to depend less on mental models can help you arrive at right decisions for everyone involved. This can help you become a better spouse, parent, and leader. It can also help you remove the emotion from decisions, which can lessen the pain of compromising a decision. Since all relationships contain many compromises, you will do better in life if you can accept compromise.

Unforced Errors

An unforced error is a mistake or wrong decision that somehow harms you. In sports, the mistake is often attributed to your failure rather than the talent of the opponent. For example, if you goof at a tennis match, you may blame yourself for not playing the right way when you were up against a better tennis player.

The fewer unforced errors you make in life, the better off you are. You can avoid making grave errors at work or in your family. You can avoid entering unhealthy relationships or losing lots of money. Things are great in life when you make wise, informed decisions.

Mental models are designed to help you avoid unforced errors. Using a first bias model, people tend to operate on loss aversion, or to prevent losses, rather than using their skills for the maximum potential benefit.

Thus, most people have a built-in loss aversion model that drives them to make decisions in life, as represented by athletes' sports decisions. This model is not ideal; however, using your maximum utility skills and focusing on making right decisions instead of minimizing losses is a better use of your energy.

Your brain has intuition, and nine times out of ten, that intuition is wrong. Many of our instincts no longer serve us, yet they run in the background, driving us to make decisions that don't make a lot of logical sense. It is wise to use your brain's intuition and mental models to guide life, not an instructional manual. If you have an intuitive response to a situation, be sure to check out your intuition with Logic before committing to the decision.

Since the brain loves to formulate predictions, you often think you know how something will go. You then base your decision off of that assumption to avoid an unforced error. However, life is seldom predictable. Take your assumptions as hypotheses, not reality.

Chapter 3: Solving Problems and Decision-Making

Traditionally speaking, we have been taught to solve a problem linearly, moving neatly from Roman numeral I to Point A. But with systems thinking, there is an acknowledgment that this isn't really how the world works: the world is messy and intertwined and unpredictable in many ways. Systems thinking urges us to look at the bigger picture, rather than the multiple components of the smaller problems and events that plague us each day. This big-picture thinking helps us to envision better solutions for complex issues.

When we talk about systems in general, we can be referring to any number of concepts, such as environmental, economic, political, social, and familial. Each of these concepts, in turn, interacts and merges to create larger systems that shape our lives: markets are created out of economic forces, both actual (companies, infrastructure) and intangible (stocks, trade regulations) coupled with political governance and social needs and desires, for example. If we simply look at a market via one conceptual lens, then we are not well equipped to understand it or to function successfully within it.

Think of the adage about teaching a man to fish. The traditional saying goes like, "I give a man a fish, and he eats for a day; if you teach a man to fish, and he eats for a lifetime." While there is something that strikes us as fundamentally correct in that saying—teaching skill is undoubtedly a longer-term solution to the problem—systems thinking requires that we look at a bigger picture. Why might the above response be inadequate?

Various other factors are present within the bigger picture. For instance, what if there aren't enough fish left in the water source because of climate change? What if the water is polluted from the activities of corporations or individuals? Who controls access to the lake, influential individuals, corporate entities, or public sources? How does the hungry man afford to buy the materials necessary to catch the fish? On the other side, what about the opportunities for expansion? Is there a local market for extra fish the man may pick? Could this be a chance at a more significant and longer-term investment?

The fact of the matter is that any of these above scenarios could occur in the bigger picture, and teaching a man to fish is only the tip of the iceberg There are all sorts of external factors that determine how adequate that response might be, not to mention personal limitations and opportunities. Systems thinking recognize that the man in this scenario, not to mention the fish, is only one small part of a much larger ecological, economic, and political universe. Acknowledging that helps us to make smarter decisions for how to create opportunities while also protecting resources.

The current challenges we face in a global world demand new and more complex answers, which requires new ways of looking at old ideas. Investing in a fossil fuel company may not be the long-term success story it once was. Relying on government intervention alone to protect resources and maintain social justice may no longer be feasible. Not to mention the straightforward fact that the above scenario changes significantly if we set the scene in, say, sub-Saharan Africa or if we consider that the fisherman might be a fisherwoman. The environmental and social challenges, not to slight the political, will differ depending on the scenario. It behooves us to examine the system and understand all the intricacies of its many dynamic parts.

Some of the benefits of systems—or bigger picture—thinking is that it encourages us to think outside of our unique skill set. We need to face challenges with multi-disciplinary zeal (which begs the question about how we educate our young adults to enter the workforce—a book in and of itself). It also, paradoxically, encourages us to make incremental rather than sweeping changes; we learn from small changes (and mistakes) and adapt accordingly. It is a more flexible way in which to approach complex problems. As we can see from the teach a man to fish analogy above, even what seems like the most straightforward problem is fraught with complex issues.

In systems thinking, there is also the implicit understanding that solving problems is not like old-style imperial conquest: you don't head off into the "wilderness" and suggest to those living and working there that your way of thinking and doing is "right" or better. Looking at the bigger picture requires considering local actors, whether they be workers or colleagues, consumers, or villagers. This kind of thinking involves facilitation, empowering localized ownership, and responsibility. This is reminiscent of some old stories—perhaps apocryphal—told about the early British colonials. In one story, missionaries descended upon an African village and, upon meeting the locals, were embarrassed and a bit horrified by their lack of what a nineteenth-century preacher would consider adequate clothing. So, they imported enough woolen suits for the men and long dresses for the women. The Africans, wishing to get along with the missionaries (who, one must not forget, were armed to the teeth), adopted the new clothes—and wore them throughout the monsoon season, with its soaking rains and soaring heat. Many villagers feel ill, and some perished. Another story, related by Jared Diamond in Guns, Germs, and Steel, talks about how colonial farmers ended up settling near waterways in Africa: this makes sense in England, where waterways provide both food and water; but in Africa, waterways are dangerous, fierce housing animals and—ultimately more deadly—large populations of mosquitoes that transmitted malaria. Before the discovery of quinine, untold numbers of settlers died of the disease. Imposing will on or ignoring wisdom from local entities is almost always disastrous.

Essentially, the more contemporary saying "act locally, think globally" could easily apply to the goals of systems thinking. Making localized changes while also revamping the system itself to be more productive and inclusive is the ideal use for more significant picture thinking. We look beyond immediate problems to long-term solutions and mobilize people from many different sectors, adapting and responding to feedback loops along the way. In the end, whether professionally or personally, this kind of thinking makes a winner out of everyone involved.

Chapter 4: Managing Chaos

Chaos Theory is concerned with explaining non-linearity in the development of systems. Analyses that are based upon a single cause seeking a single effect are linear. Non-linearity represents unpredictable change. Change, in turn, means that a system is dynamic. Lack of change denotes a static system. Systems rarely operate in a steady-state and progress in a linear fashion. A linear system is deterministic; its outcomes can be predicted from the initial conditions, cause, and effect. However, it is much more common for the form of a system to change unpredictably. As a system, a tree will develop from seed to seedling, from sapling to maturity, old age, limb loss, and die back. Its general form or genotype will be mostly predictable, but its specific shape or phenotype will not. Indeed, every tree, although similar within species, will be different. No two trees, dogs, cats, cows, landscapes, cloud formations, snowflakes in a snowstorm, or people on earth will be the same. A car will run well when new, but over time, paint fades, rust will invade, bearings will wear out, and parts will fail. No two old cars, even of the same make and model, will be the same. A perusal of quality and prices of stock of secondhand car dealers will suffice to prove this point.

Similarly, a human will change over his/her lifetime as youthful strength and agility may decline. Still, thinking and rational capacity may increase until all sub-systems break down in old age. Therefore, systems do not move through time with precisely the same shape as when they commenced. If they made it, their progress would be linear. But systems development is non-linear. The development of Chaos theory helps to explain non-linearity.

Chaos does not represent disorder. Instead it explains that there is the order in what at first sight appears to be disorder. Each tree in the forest is different, representing disorder, but the differences lie within predictable bounds as each one is recognizably a tree. This represents the order in the seeming disorder. The characteristics of Chaos are:

- Sensitivity to initial conditions (as mentioned above about system creation) leads to unpredictability.

- Mixing in which adjacent points may end up in entirely different positions as the system progresses.

- Non-linearity as the output of one system becomes the input to the preceding one.

- Feedback is a significant driver of Chaos.

The concept of increasing order within a system may be traced to Descartes. Descartes held that the ordinary laws of nature would bring about order and that an external guiding hand was unnecessary.

A feature of systems is wholeness. But paradoxically, within the wholeness lies further complexity as systems are formed of sub-systems. While these sub-systems are 'whole,' they, in turn, are components of the larger system. And not only are the more extensive system components, but they often do not have a viable independent existence and are in themselves composed of further subordinate sub-systems. For example, the trunk of a tree is an essential component of the system that is a tree but, once removed, ceases to function independently. The sub-system of the tree trunk consists of subordinate sub-systems of Bark to provide protection, Phloem to supply sap from leaves to branches and roots, Cambium to provide new cells for the phloem, Xylem to move water and minerals up the tree to the leaves, and Heartwood that consists of old Xylem and provides support and strength. Each of these can be analyzed down the level of the individual cells that comprise them. The same analysis may be conducted with a cow's liver or the gearbox of a motor car. They exist in themselves but are, in turn, comprised of further sub-systems. The origins of the word system can be seen: 'system' is Latin for a whole consisting of several parts. Therefore, a system is a group of components that interact to form an integrated entity or whole.

An economy is a system as it takes in raw materials, transforms them by production processes into goods and services, and distributes them for consumption. Therefore, the Economic System analysis involves studying the production, exchange, and consumption of goods and services. The economic system's foundation structure may be depicted in its broad sub-system components of production, exchange, and consumption.

Chapter 5: Creating Lasting Solutions

Traditionally speaking, we have been taught to solve a problem linearly, moving neatly from Roman numeral I to Point A. But with systems thinking, there is an acknowledgment that this isn't really how the world works: the world is messy and intertwined and unpredictable in many ways. Systems thinking urges us to look at the bigger picture, rather than the multiple components of the smaller problems and events that plague us each day. This big-picture thinking helps us to envision better solutions for complex issues.

When we talk about systems in general, we can be referring to any number of concepts, such as environmental, economic, political, social, and familial. Each of these concepts, in turn, interacts and merges to create larger systems that shape our lives: markets are created out of economic forces, both actual (companies, infrastructure) and intangible (stocks, trade regulations) coupled with political governance and social needs and desires, for example. If we simply look at a market via one conceptual lens, we cannot understand it or function successfully.

Think of the adage about teaching a man to fish. The traditional saying goes like, "I give a man a fish, and he eats for a day; if you teach a man to fish, and he eats for a lifetime." While there is something that strikes us as fundamentally correct in that saying—teaching skill is undoubtedly a longer-term solution to the problem—systems thinking requires that we look at a bigger picture. Why might the above response be inadequate?

Various other factors are present within the bigger picture. For instance, what if there aren't enough fish left in the water source because of climate change? What if the water is polluted from the activities of corporations or individuals? Who controls access to the lake, influential individuals, corporate entities, or public sources? How does the hungry man afford to buy the materials necessary to catch the fish? On the other side, what about the expansion opportunities? Is there a local market for extra fish the man may pick? Could this be a chance at a more significant and longer-term investment?

The fact of the matter is that any of these above scenarios could occur in the bigger picture, and teaching a man to fish is only the tip of the iceberg.

There are all sorts of external factors that determine how adequate that response might be, not to mention personal limitations and opportunities. Systems thinking recognizes that the man in this scenario, not to mention the fish, is only one small part of a much larger ecological, economic, and political universe. Acknowledging that helps us to make smarter decisions for how to create opportunities while also protecting resources.

The current challenges we face in a global world demand new and more complex answers, which requires new ways of looking at old ideas. Investing in a fossil fuel company may not be the long-term success story it once was. Relying on government intervention alone to protect resources and maintain social justice may no longer be feasible. Not to mention the straightforward fact that the above scenario changes significantly if we set the scene in, say, sub-Saharan Africa or if we consider that the fisherman might be a fisherwoman. The environmental and social challenges, not to slight the political, will differ depending on the scenario. It behooves us to examine the system and understand all the intricacies of its many dynamic parts.

One of the benefits of systems—or more significant picture—thinking is that it encourages us to think outside of our unique skill set. We need to face challenges with multi-disciplinary zeal (which begs how we educate our young adults to enter the workforce—a book in and of itself). Paradoxically, it encourages us to make incremental rather than sweeping changes; we learn from small changes (and mistakes) and adapt accordingly. It is a more flexible way in which to approach complex problems. As we can see from the teach a man to fish analogy above, even what seems like the most straightforward problem is fraught with complex issues.

In systems thinking, there is also the implicit understanding that solving problems is not like old-style imperial conquest: you don't head off into the "wilderness" and suggest to those living and working there that your way of thinking and doing is "right" or better. Looking at the bigger picture requires considering local actors, whether they be workers or colleagues, consumers, or villagers. This kind of thinking involves facilitation, empowering localized ownership, and responsibility. This is reminiscent of some old stories—perhaps apocryphal—told about the early British colonials. In one story, missionaries descended upon an African village and, upon meeting the locals, were embarrassed and a bit horrified by their lack of what a nineteenth-century preacher would consider adequate clothing. So, they imported enough woolen suits for the men and long dresses for the women. The Africans, wishing to get along with the missionaries (who, one must not forget, were armed to the teeth), adopted the new clothes—and wore them throughout the monsoon season, with its soaking rains and soaring heat. Many villagers feel ill, and some perished. Another story, related by Jared Diamond in Guns, Germs, and Steel, talks about how colonial farmers ended up settling near waterways in Africa: this makes sense in England, where waterways provide both food and water; but in Africa, waterways are dangerous, fierce housing animals and—ultimately more deadly—large populations of mosquitoes that transmitted malaria. Before the discovery of quinine, untold numbers of settlers died of the disease. Imposing will on or ignoring wisdom from local entities is almost always disastrous.

The newer saying "act locally, think globally" could easily apply to systems thinking goals. Making localized changes while also revamping the system itself to be more productive and inclusive is ideal for more significant picture thinking. We look beyond immediate problems to long-term solutions and mobilize people from many different sectors, adapting and responding to feedback loops along the way. In the end, whether professionally or personally, this kind of thinking makes a winner out of everyone involved.

Chapter 6: Know Yourself through Thought patterns

Remove Negative Influences Cut Off Destroying Thoughts

Negative energy is everywhere. You can find it at every turn. Negative energy can take the form of unhappy people, violent content on television, or even environmental damage. You can see this consistently. No matter where you go, you will encounter charges of negative energy.

And while there isn't much, you can do to stop negative energy from swirling around in the world, and there is plenty that you can do to stop it from taking over your mind. When you find yourself immersed in a hostile environment, it is straightforward to get caught up in the situation's negativity.

For instance, you are working in a very hostile environment. Your boss and co-workers aren't getting along, which leads to an overall unpleasant atmosphere. At this point, you have one of two choices, you either let that get to you, or you don't. Of course, it's not quite that simple.

One of the most effective ways to avoid being brought down by this type of atmosphere is to stop it from getting to you merely. You can learn to recognize the onset of negative thoughts and emotions. When you do, you can nip them in the bud. You can make use of mantras such as "negative energies can't touch me" or "negative thoughts are like a ship passing in the night."

In other words, don't let negative thoughts pull up a chair and have a seat. If you allow them to do that, you are opening the door to trouble. The main thing to keep in mind is that you are the master of your thoughts and emotions. The only way something can get to you is if you let it.

However, indeed, a highly hostile environment will undoubtedly charge you with negative energy. In that case, it is always a great idea to have ways in which you can unload those energies. That is why pleasant activities are needed at the end of the day. That way, you can simply let go of the energies which are negatively affecting you.

Secrets to Successfully Tame Your Thoughts

If people knew that succeeding in life depended on their actions, they would be less likely to worry about their lives. At times, we go through life with regrets and anxiety. We don't feel ready to let go of the feelings that we have embedded within us. Concerning our future, we worry about tomorrow, but a large number of people don't know the power that they have. The power that you have within you can quickly become a destructive force or a constructive force that will push you to succeed in life. You have the power to control your life and live it as you wish. What you think about is what you become. If you keep thinking that you will always struggle in life, rest assured that you will struggle to keep things afloat. Conversely, if you genuinely believe that everything will fall into place and that your time will come for you to enjoy life, expect to live a life full of optimism.

Listen to Yourself

To tame your thoughts, start by listening to yourself. Do this as though you were explaining something to other people. How would you want to tell other people about the story of your life? Without a doubt, you would want to talk about everything that you have done well. No one would want to tell others negative stories about themselves. Therefore, you should adopt a similar attitude when listening to yourself. Focus on treating yourself with the same respect that you would expect from other people. This means that you should strive to focus on thoughts that put you in a positive light.

Your Inner Self is Listening

Besides, you should always bear in mind that your inner self is listening to your thoughts; this is the inner you. So, if you continue thinking about negative things, your inner self will listen and conform to how you expect it to behave. When thinking positively, it will also listen to you and adapt to help you perceive life with optimism. Therefore, before blaming other people for the bad things that are happening to you, remember that there is someone within you who is listening to your self-talk.

Befriend Your Emotional Guidance System

The point here is that you should pause every time you notice that your emotions have changed. You should take some time to evaluate your emotions and the next thoughts before they gain momentum. The effect of this is that it will help you develop an attitude of thinking twice before doing anything. Before doing anything, you will reflect on whether what you're about to do is favorable or not. You increase the likelihood of making the right decisions without allowing emotions to cloud your judgment.

Find Your Stop Signs

Another practical tip that can make a difference in how you think is visualizing stop signs that signal to you that you should stop thinking about something. Your stop signs will warrant that you regain your senses and avoid thinking about your past or worrying about your future. The best way of using these stop signs is to remind you that your thoughts are not helping to build you up. For instance, you can come up with a stop sign that reminds you that you are overthinking about events that prevent you from being happy. It might take some time for you to master how to use these stop signs, but the outcome will be rewarding as it will enhance your self-awareness.

Consider Words as Your Nutrition

When thinking about improving our health, we know perfectly that eating right can only be done. The foods that you choose to eat have an impact on your health. In the same manner, the words that float around in your mind impact your mental health. This means that it is essential that you control the information that you feed into your mind. For example, watching horrific content on television might not be as entertaining as you think. In the long run, this will harm how you think and the thoughts that frequent your mind.

Remind Yourself with Affirmations

Becoming the master of your mind also demands that you stay on top of your game. You have to keep yourself engaged in festive gear. Sure, there are instances when you might slip up and think negatively, but with the right affirmations, you will feel unstoppable. Have these affirmations in areas where you can easily see them. Pin them next to your files in your office. Before going to bed, remind yourself of your higher purpose by reading out these affirmations to yourself. They can eliminate anxiety and soothe you to sleep better.

Take Out the Trash

Increasing your self-awareness about your thoughts will give you the advantage of identifying unnecessary thoughts and emotions. When you do this steadily, you will find it easier to declutter your mind. The notion of taking out the trash shouldn't drive you to overthink about your past. Instead, the point here is to develop an attitude where you simply admit that some thoughts are not worth holding on to. Practice meditation exercises as a method of increasing your self-awareness. This is the best way of raising your antennas high enough to pick any signals of unwanted thoughts in your mind.

Pursue Meaning Over Pleasure

There is a good reason why you should strive to be happy. Most people have never realized that there are adverse effects of focusing too much on striving for positivity. Sure, we all want our lives to be full of happiness. However, we should come to terms with the fact that too much of anything is detrimental. This also applies to happiness. When we go about chasing happiness, we surround ourselves with all the things that can keep us entertained and full of joy. The downside of this kind of life is that it can blind us to unrealistic optimism.

Flex Your Muscle Memory

Technology has changed the way we access information in today's world. The digital devices that we have been introduced to make it easy for us to consume information than ever before. However, this affects our muscle memory since we rely too much on these devices. You can find Millennials struggling with simple calculations where they have to turn to their smartphones. According to a study, to some extent, seniors from the Baby Boomer generation have better memory compared to Millennials.

Chapter 7: Take Control Over Your Thought Patterns

A "controlled thinking" mindset helps you to shift your focus intentionally. It allows you to determine your performance, rather than getting stuck replaying negative experiences in your head. You have to purposefully choose to focus on what you want instead.

In order to choose where you want to put your attention, you need to take control of your mind, thoughts, and emotions. You are only as stuck or as free as your mindset allows you to be. It is the story of good or bad experiences your mind tells you. It is the story of your life. It is the imprint of your mind.

The mind is an incredible machine. When given the right kind of input, it can produce amazing results. It is a habitual learner. It wants to adapt to its environment, including whatever patterns of thoughts, emotions, and actions you expose it to. It can also adapt to change. As its owner, you have the power to rewrite the story. You can choose to override the negative, limiting thoughts and emotions. You can decide to tell a different story and one that will empower you. You must intentionally choose to change your thinking and take control of your life.

To shift your mindset, you must first identify your habitual thoughts and emotions and then learn to shift them intentionally (not simply by willpower) by creating a better story.

You take control of where you focus your attention. You can choose to think or you can choose to feel. When you choose to think and feel the right things, you take control of your story, you write a different ending, and you define your life.

The key to transformation lies in you. It all starts with the story your mind tells you. Your mind is defined by your thoughts and emotions. You are a habitual thinker. You do not typically think of something once and decide to never think about it again. Your thoughts initiative your emotions which in turn shape your responses and behaviors. Because your mind is a "habitual" learner, it will automatically and repetitively go to the place where you decide to take it.

You take control of where you focus your attention. You can choose to think or you can choose to feel. When you choose to think and feel the right things, you take control of your story, you write a different ending, and you define your life.

Your thinking story is defined by your subconscious beliefs, patterns, pictures, and stories. As the writer of this story, you can change it. It exists in your mind, and with some shifts of your thinking, you can change it.

The statement: "I cannot" does not exist in reality. It only has a place in your thoughts and emotions, and you can change your mind about it. Do not repeat this kind of thinking. You can change it. You can move past it, and you can coach yourself to think something that is more empowering. You can accept and you can look for the right meaning. You can choose to feel the way you choose to feel. You can choose to think and feel the way that is best for you.

When you change your mindset, you not only change your life, but you change your reality. It is all in your mind. You can change your life story and let it move you positively.

The mind is a powerful thing. It drives your reality. It can be a powerful friend or a formidable foe, depending on the thoughts you choose to follow. It will help you to thrive if you allow it to. It will keep you stuck if you let it get in the way.

As the main character in your story, you have the power to tell your own story, to write your own destiny. You are the master of your mind. You can choose to create whatever you want. You control your thoughts and your emotions. You ARE in control of your life.

Chapter 8: Logic and Analytical Thinking

Now we addressed the question: what are methodological competencies? Now, we may wonder, how do you profit from System Thinking skills?

Enhancing your System Thinking skills isn't a small feat; it has several benefits to become a more effective problem solver: analytical abilities make you marketable: this is one of the most measurable and practical benefits of enhancing your analytics and System Thinking skills.

With the improvement of each of the above analytical skills, you would be more marketable, hirable at once.

Now, if you have your dream work already, fantastic! Learning these skills will help you shine in your employer's eyes and allow you to work better in less time.

Nonetheless, learning how to develop System Thinking skills will help you achieve this role you were looking for if you don't have your dream job.

Glide into your CV a few analytical skills, and your future boss will be very impressed.

Analytical skills help you solve the problem better: an effective imaginative problem solver lets you quickly tackle even the most daunting cognitive issues. In reality, when you know how data can be digested, the relevant information extracted, and a creative solution created, nothing can stand in the way and what you want.

Practical problem-solving at home, at work, or for a personal project would motivate you to succeed tomorrow.

Strategic thinking is encouraged through analytical skills: What is System Thinking? It is a type of intellectual discipline that emphasizes rational knowledge synthesis to generate informed thought and action.

It means we can interact with knowledge, experience, and even other people without reacting so often. The more conscious, the less reactive, we love, we love. And as we begin to think objectively, we pave the way for stronger interpersonal relationships.

In this stage of the problem-solving dilemma, the brain gathers the information that will later give us the tools to create a resolution to the problem at hand. It is always seeking information. The information coming into the brain starts to be organized and shuffled to make sense of what the outside world is doing. At this stage, mostly what is happing is just getting the information, assessing the situation, and looking for an answer to the problem.

Analytical thinking uses the sense to gather information. A person has been transported to a hospital after a severe car accident. The emergency room nurse will evaluate the person and ask questions to gather information to improve the patient's health and current situation. Watching vitals and how the patient is responding to different evaluations will determine how the nurse will take the steps needed to save this patient's life. Analytical thinking gathers the information in the world so the brain can determine the solution to the current problem.

A great way to create a more vital analytical thinking skill is to practice. The walkout in the world and just observe the surroundings. Be mindful of what is going on, look at details, and notice your interest. Create questions about how things work and understand the concept. Games are another great way to improve the analytical mind. Research online and find brain games that will help you improve your brain function. When resolving a problem, look at the pros and cons of the issue. Be intentional in your decision making and recognize the consequences of your decision.

How to Develop Analytical Thinking Skills in 5 Easy Steps

Would it not apply to become a more strategic thinker with more robust analytical skills? Working to improve and develop your analytical skills will certainly not hurt!

Below are a few steps to begin developing more vital analytical skills: Play brain games: It is a fun and realistic way to get started to improve your analytical abilities and increase your brain capacity. So 15 minutes a day is what you need!

An ideal way to continue improving your System Thinking skills is to download a brain training app to test your cognitive skills.

You can access several approved applications to develop your analytical skills:

- Luminosity

- Elevate

- Eidetic

- Wizard

- Happily

- Brain Wave

Each day, learn something new: make it your habit to learn something new every day.

Most of us, once completed with education, are much more passive in our research. We read when we need to, we learn new skills, but we never try emotional and cognitive stimulation entirely by ourselves.

Ok, strive to know something that excites your passions every day. Go online and look for a topic that has always fascinated you. Speak to an expert in a field in which you are interested. Go out and broaden your knowledge base the day before by knowing something you didn't know.

Therefore, not only can you read more by entering the book club, but you can also participate in direct review and discussion at book club meetings. You have the opportunity to discuss the theoretical study, analyze metaphors and unpack symbolism.

And you can even make some friends in the process!

Volunteering in new projects: If you are interested in a particular analytical ability, why not volunteer for a project involving this ability?

Sometimes, we need a little inner drive to get into something different. We can't wait for anything in our lap yet. We must to be able to go out there and do it ourselves every once and a while.

If you want to learn new analytical skills to apply to your arsenal, volunteer for projects and activities to bring you through the training first!

Take an online course: first, you will determine what appeals to you the most if you want to develop your analytical skills.

Endure in mind that you may already have some of the above analytical skills. Everyone has different strengths and weaknesses, so it is essential to decide where you lie.

Why? And if we follow what we already know, we only can't discover something new — or do any favors for ourselves.

If you want to develop your analytical arsenal, you have to try something you haven't learned yet.

Perhaps you would like to develop your research skills. Perhaps you may like to try your hand in data processing and reporting.

If you like, do some work to see what can be found online.

You will take an in-person course nearby. And you may sign up to obtain distance education from your home comfort.

You will take a constructive approach to develop your analytical skills. So, decide for yourself what you want, and go for it!

Your passion for success is the secret to growing your System Thinking skills and developing your analytical skills.

You can prepare yourself for tomorrow's triumphs, but only if you find the door to go through can you take the appropriate steps to open it.

Each of us can do unique and beautiful things.

So, what would you like to do with your future? The person you want to be is all about focused, deliberate action.

Think about where you want to change the most. Define your weaknesses, define your strengths. Find your strengths, find your weaknesses. And become more vital than you ever dreamed of before.

Chapter 9: Critical Thinking

Critical thinking helps us with different data. It may help us think. One way to approach thinking is through the Analysis of Logic--such as formal Logic (which assembles decisions almost mathematically (with syllogisms), simple Logic (which also considers material, context, and delivery), and fuzzy Logic (which admits that lots of attributes are subjective or topics of level). Critical thinking provides us with strategies to think through data and a way to decide which opinions are important. One might manipulate data to change information in various ways. In fact, computer programs change data. Yet some would argue that manipulation brings an uncertain kind of knowledge.

There's always further information related to data, and these issues have various meanings. Information could have various purposes. One of the most important aspects perhaps is that data doesn't decide anything, but instead models our understanding. Another important aspect is that data is merely information, not knowledge. Another aspect of data is that it's useless if we can't deal with the information. Yet another important aspect is that data's seriousness stays steady, remaining above fluff and gossip.

This story is a rational story. Scientists are logical. Critical thinkers will also find it logical. Yet, not everybody thinks rationally. Rational thoughts may not be free. Rational thought may be the consequence of skills acquired, like any other skills. We use skills because we need them, for example in a functional life. Critical thinking counts more than critical analysis.

In this story, there are many questions, not all of which have concrete answers, although we may try to understand what all those data mean. In fact, the story raises many questions, because questions create wonder and self-reflection.

A critical thinker asks questions, but also uses barriers to excess curiosity. That is, a critical thinker lets the data speak, and doesn't try to put the information into an uneasy package where it doesn't fit. A few data are like a weak light in a dark room.

This is a story about other options people often don't consider. One character takes one particular option. He is alone in seeking it, and it isn't always so clear what he is seeking. He is a clear, creative thinker who questions the anomalous. He is a philosopher-scientist. This story is concerned with some of the stuff philosophy and science have considered. Still, we may need to discover what's essential for a creative life on earth.

The character in this story is often lonely, but he doesn't mind. In fact, it's his solitude that allows his mind to work. This character has the courage to think the unusual and the skill to dwell on the questions and ideas his critical thinking produces. One character talks of him in these words: "Well done, John. Well done. I'm surprised at your insight. I'm doubly surprised, your insight is original. Very few people come up with ideas like this one. You have a unique mind. I'm impressed--John. " In general, the character in this story is an original genius. But, he understands that his ideas haven't prevailed, and he's aware of history.

The character in this story seems unusual. In fact, the character may seem at first to avoid traditional goals in life. In the end, the character does achieve what he's after. The character receives acclaim for his work. The character works hard throughout the story, as the story itself demonstrates.

For this reason, his goal of reasoning may seem worthwhile because pieces of it show up in different places. Also, he's been successful in his speech, because he's well-spoken. He's articulate. This is a story of a rational man, a man who thinks at length and with clarity. He answers his questions, and also makes questions. He gives answers, and presents new questions. This man with a unique mind struggles to achieve the clarity of mind which is his dream.

This story provides data, not just its usual telling of a story. Challenging, original data makes up the story, like most of the things we care to know about.

When we think, we're not only logical in how we do it, but also creative, and critical, and even emotional. We think with our imagination. And such thoughts may go in unexpected directions.

Science is a good example of how to be logical and inventive. Critical thinking is a way to development insight. Philosophy allows us to think. Our minds need more than we often give them. This is a story of one man who thinks. This man thinks a lot. He doesn't mind being alone. This man thinks. He thinks the impossible, too. He considers things like teleportation and how to know what will happen in certain situations. This man who thinks and thinks and thinks has a passion for thinking. In the end, we see this man is a free thinker who often sees things in new ways, and he enjoys his work in cryptography and also general research.

More than anything else, this man thinks. He thinks about the science that surrounds him. And he thinks about life. He thinks about the future. He thinks about time and about how the future and the past exist in different kinds of ways. He thinks about time travel, too, including what it's like and how it might be possible. He also thinks about philosophy, and about critical thinking itself. He thinks about anomalous data, and he thinks about data itself. He thinks about the nature of data. Are data changing as they age, over time?

Chapter 10: What is Critical Thinking?

Critical thinking can be defined as thinking and being rational about your beliefs or what to do. It involves the ability of one to engage in independent and reflective thinking. A person with critical thinking skills should be able to do the following:

Objectively reflect on why their beliefs and values are justified;

Systematically solve problems;

Understand the connection between ideas logically;

Identify, construct, understand, and analyze arguments;

Identify inconsistent mistakes in reasoning; and

Understand the importance and relevance of ideas.

Critical thinking can also be described as the skill to analyze facts to conclude logically. It involves careful consideration of information established as accurate, clearly outlining a rational process of thought about that information, and objectively arriving at a judgment.

If that last paragraph sounds complicated, the good news is that you have probably already engaged in some form of critical thinking.

If you want to purchase a new car and know what you want regarding the car's price, condition, quality, and features, you have to compare several different car models. You might read several reviews about a particular car that seems like the right one. You'll collect more information about that specific car. If it fits your criteria, you'll then compare sellers in terms of their pricing and customer feedback to find a seller that you can trust to give you the right car at a reasonable price. Along the way, you'll make sure that the reviews you are reading come from reliable sources that honestly describe the car and the seller (rather than old reviews that may no longer reflect current conditions, reviews that don't explain anything, or biased reviews that might not reflect an accurate assessment). Once you have analyzed the facts, you find the right car model and seller and ultimately make your purchase.

You just used a form of critical thinking to purchase a car. You had a clear purpose (finding a car), you came up with a solution (you decided which model of the car you wanted to buy), you used information (reviews) while carefully determining which information was truthful and useful (only using reviews you trusted), analyzed that information, and solved your problem (you now have a new car).

You did NOT merely pick a car that looked nice in the photographs and went to the first car dealership you found one random day. You also didn't just take every review at face value or buy a specific car because someone told you to buy that one. You

You not only thought about your decision and used the information to come to it, but you also thought about why you were making that particular choice and put some thought into the information in front of you.

Of course, sifting through all of those reviews, prices, and feedback is time-consuming and not always straightforward. Suppose you are trying to decide upon which political candidate to vote for, which college you should attend, or some other decision that may involve your own personal values, the process of critical thinking can be even more complicated. In that case, thus, this book will help you understand critical thinking as a tool for everyday life as well as the "big questions" you may come across.

It is important to note that critical thinking is not about the accumulation of information. If a person has an excellent memory or is aware of many facts, it does not mean that they are critical thinkers. A critical thinker is an individual that can realize the consequences from the information they have and understands how to effectively use the information they have to solve problems and seek more relevant information to stay informed.

Being argumentative or critical of others is now what critical thinking is all about. Critical thinking skills can be used to point out fallacies and wrong reasoning and play a role in joint reasoning and constructive improvements and tasks. Critical thinking can also be used to improve work processes and enhance social institutions.

It has been argued that critical thinking obstructs creativity because it involves following the rules of rationality and logic, while creativity may involve breaking the same rules. However, this is not true. Critical thinking is very compatible with many aspects of creative thinking. In essence, critical thinking is an essential part of creativity, as we require critical thinking to evaluate and enhance creative ideas.

Skills in Critical Thinking

Critical thinking is a lifelong process that even the most profound thinkers continuously practice and refine further. Think about the following skills less like something you can just suddenly perfect and more like habits of mind that you'll always take with you—habits that will improve over time. Regardless of your origin or background, it is essential to have critical thinking skills. The lack of such skills can break one's career due to the inability to understand and analyze information effectively.

In this era of immense competition, critical thinking skills are more critical than ever before. According to Kris Potrafka, everything is at risk—thus the need to think more critically. Lack of critical thinking will lessen your chances of climbing the ladder in your career or industry of choice. In order not to succumb to such, it is essential to develop your skills in critical thinking. However, it is essential first to understand what those skills are to know how to improve or enhance them.

There are no universal standards for the skills required in critical thinking, but in this section, we shall discuss six of them:

Identification

Firstly, you need to determine what's wrong and what influenced this to happen. Only through understanding your circumstance can you solve your problem.

Once you have identified the problem or situation, you need to stop and take a mental inventory of what is going on as you inquire:

What is being done?

What caused your situation?

What will likely happen?

Research

When comparing the different aspects of a situation or an issue, uninfluenced research ability is essential. Arguments must be convincing. This means that the figures and facts presented may be lacking in context or are not credible.

To help with this, verify the unsourced claims. Is the person bringing the argument offering their source of information? If you ask and there is no clear answer, that should serve as a warning. Learn to verify the sources of any information and its authenticity.

Identify biases

This is a difficult skill. It is not easy to recognize a bias, yet it is very crucial in critical thinking. Strong critical thinkers must be objective in evaluating the information they receive. Take the assumption that you are a judge required to listen to both sides and keep in mind the biases on both sides.

Of equal importance, however, if not more, is learning how you must set aside your own biases so that your judgment is impartial. Learn to debate and argue with your thoughts and perceptions. This is important as a skill because it enables you to see things from different viewpoints.

Always assess your source of information and challenge the evidence that forms your beliefs. You must always be aware of the existence of biases. As you analyze any information or argument, it is essential to ask yourself the following questions:

Who benefits?

The source of information—is it credible, or does it have a hidden agenda?

Is the source biased and overlooks details proving them wrong?

Is it persuasive enough to let make people believe?

Inference

The ability to internalize and make conclusions based on available information is also essential in mastering critical thinking. Most of the information won't mean it as is. As a critical thinker, you will often need to analyze the information presented and come up with conclusions based on raw data.

It is not easy to infer. An inference is an informed guess, and the ability to correctly infer can be enhanced by consciously making an effort to collect as much information as you possibly can before you jump to conclusions.

Determine Relevance

Critical thinking can be very challenging when figuring out what information is most relevant to analyze. In many cases, you may be presented with information that may seem very important only to realize that it is a minor point to consider.

The best solution to determine relevance is to first understand what is expected. Have you been asked to find a solution? Should you understand the trend? When you understand what is expected from the situation, it becomes much easier to know what is relevant and what is not.

Another tip to determining the relevance of information is by making a list of data points that you rank to be relevant. In doing this, you will likely have a list containing relevant information at the top of the list and not so important information down. Then, trim down these details and put your attention to what's relevant.

Curiosity

It is a more comfortable choice to accept every piece of information presented at face value. However, this can be disastrous when faced with a situation that requires thinking critically. Every human being is naturally curious. Don't allow the impulse to ask questions to die because that is not the way of critical thinkers.

Train yourself to be productively curious. Asking insightful questions about your daily reality necessitates mindfulness, and it's a vital ability you must acquire as a critical thinker.

Chapter 11:   Critical Thinking for Change your Life

Critical thinking is an ability that can be applied to every area of one's everyday life. You might be shocked at the decisions you can, will, and have made, requiring you to think critically before following through. Critical thinking is more than logic and reason. It is also a process of information gathering, which involves gathering and assessing information and thinking about your thinking.

"Critical thinking" is actually a very simple process, but it's also a very powerful one. You are the user of critical thinking; you are its instrument. There is a critical thinking method; every critical thinker uses and employs it in his or her own way.

People actually think critically and use critical thinking without realizing it. Sometimes we call it "enlightened common sense."

We all regularly asked to think critically in our lives. Important decisions await our judgment and our action; time for reflection is short. Critical thinking is a skill that can help us to deal with such cases and situations.

The skill of critical thinking will allow us to better solve problems, deal with irrational and ill-advised decisions, and make better, more informed, decisions in all areas of our lives. Let's try to understand what critical thinking is.

To understand what critical thinking is, let's first talk about what it is not. Critical thinking is not brain surgery, and it is not a discipline taught in school.

Consider, for example, what is required to be a neurosurgeon: You must spend years of study and training. With this formalized training you will develop a complex expertise.

In comparison, a skill in critical thinking has a different history. There is no formal training regimen or certification process. This skill is basically a skill of the mind, but it must rely on at least two disciplines for its creation, training, and development. Those two disciplines are logic and philosophy.

It takes both logic and philosophy to train the mind to think critically. It doesn't have to be through formal education, but that's the best way to learn.

Consider the following as a definition of critical thinking: "Critical thinking is a skill for identifying biases in the way you think that can cause you to reach invalid conclusions." Armed with a skill in critical thinking

You can perform critical thinking at any time. A lot of people have questioned the efficiency of critical thinking, ranging from people who haven't read about it or experienced it and think it is just a bunch of book-learning, to people who have read about it and seen how effective it can be, but cannot apply it in their lives.

This is due to lack of practice and skills in this area. Critical thinking is not as easy to learn as some other skills are. It does take practice, but the more you practice, the easier it becomes. Improvement in one's critical thinking skills does not have to be slow or difficult.

We not only need to know what critical thinking is, we need to know what it is not. The skill has been greatly misunderstood, and it has been severely underestimated. Some say that it is a concept taught in classrooms. That is not true.

Critical thinking is a skill that is needed throughout everyday life. Our daily lives often present us with opportunities to judge and make decisions. It is quite easy to make a poor decision, requiring us to waste time and money, because of bias or haste.

Critical thinking can be used just to make life easier and easier. It does not take much time or effort, but the results are often impressive. Critical thinking allows us to approach a problem without bias.

In other words, we want to become an impartial decision maker who is considering all the evidence before making a decision, even if we might not have all the necessary facts. Critical thinking allows us to make wiser and more informed decisions.

I expect that you will be involved in some of these decisions. You might find yourself making a very important decision, perhaps one that will have a direct impact on the rest of your life, such as choosing a college, choosing a life partner, business partner, or even a friend.

Maybe you're just making a snap judgment. With critical thinking, you can make the best decision without resorting to snap judgments. Critical thinking leads us to a judgment that will be based on careful reasoning. It will be the best decision until new information is collected that causes you to change your decision.

Critical thinking gives us the chance to make the best informed decision. Our decisions must be based on the judgments that result from careful reasoning. Further, your judgment must consider all the relevant arguments.

Chapter 12:   Critical Reading

Learning to read critically involves actively participating in what we read, first developing a clear understanding of the author's ideas, then challenging and evaluating the arguments and evidence provided to support those arguments, and finally forming our points of view. In this way, reading requires us to develop skills that are not necessary for more passive forms of information retrieval.

Steps for Critical Reading:

• Before reading

scan the piece to get an idea of what it is and the main argument. It can include reading an introduction, if available, or captions.

• As you read

continue an ongoing dialogue with the author through comments, recording your thoughts, ideas, and questions. Underline, feature, or circle significant parts and points and compose remarks in the margins.

- After reading

check their remarks to get an overall thought of the content. You can likewise decide to write a summary to improve your comprehension.

- If you react to the text after you have built up a clear sense of the author's argument and thinking

you can dissect the author's argument and techniques. At that point, you can build up your thoughts, perhaps in your display.

Reading critically means that the reader is always thinking. The reader makes judgment calls about what is going on in the text by asking questions. They notice clues and make inferences. A reader who is critical can figure out what the author's purpose is and how the writer is using language to persuade the reader to do something.

When a person reads a text, they're looking for the main purpose of the text. A critical reader asks questions that help them figure out where the author is going with the text. Just like a detective, a critical reader asks questions and looks for clues.

Clues are pieces of information an author has put into the text. Critical readers look for clues in the beginning of the text because usually the beginning will give clues about what's coming up.

The ending of the story provides clues about what is to come. Reading critically means that the reader is always thinking. This gives the reader the opportunity to make predictions about what is going to happen.

For example, they are thinking:

"Based on this information, I'm guessing what the next event is going to be."

A critical reader asks questions that let them see their hunches were right or wrong. Questions that a critical reader asks can be about details, logical thoughts, or about the author's purpose. Critical readers

Critical reading is the process of doing close reading of a text, known as a text analysis. When doing a text analysis, the reader is looking for certain details in the text. Critical reading is hard work. A person who does a text analysis looks for details that help show the author's purpose. The person who is doing an analysis tries to figure out the writer's purpose for writing the text.

In this story the main purpose of the writing is to entertain the reader. The story has several points and each point adds to this main purpose. This story is an adventure story with a great plot and strong characters. This story will keep the reader actively involved, and encourage the reader to keep reading until the end.

Once the student has read the story and asked the questions, they will be ready to answer the questions by an analysis of the story. The kind of questions that a critical reader asks will help to create the analysis. Once the reader has read the story, they will create an initial draft of their analysis. Then they will

The initial draft is a first draft. It is a rough draft to get the main ideas out. Once the main ideas are out, they should try to refine it. This is the process of getting the ideas and making them fit together in a logical way.

They may make changes to the draft along the way. If they have questions about parts of the draft, they will ask someone who is familiar with the story, perhaps the teacher or an older sibling. They will ask these people if

the draft makes sense.

Personal experiences are an important key to making the draft better.

Personal experiences are things that relate to how the person feels towards

the story. The reader can use them

if the person reads, enjoys reading, if the plot of the story is relatable, and

if the character in the story

Chapter 13:   Critical Writing

Writing critically is very important in academic writing. In your English classes, you will be asked to write at least one argumentative paper that will ask you to defend one side or another. Critical writing can be broken down. To put it merely, critical writing evaluates and analyzes more than one source to develop an argument. This is different than descriptive writing, which describes what something is like. However, a description will be involved in your critical writing, along with an explanation. There should be a right balance between analysis and description. Critical thinking will make your writing clearer and more concise. This allows you to make well-thought-out arguments in a shorter amount of time with more success. Being transparent will increase readability. This will allow for a wider audience and a more enjoyable read. When writing, sometimes it is difficult to put your thoughts on paper without sounding crazy. Being told to write more clearly is a lot easier than actually writing clearly. Therefore, this is going to give you a few tips and pointers on becoming a better writer.

At this point, you have heard a lot about how to think critically, cognitive biases, and how to escape the trap Groupthink creates. Now, you will be able to write critically. When you are writing critically, you'll be able to word your thoughts better, and your paragraphs will be more useful – it won't just be about word counts anymore, but the word counts will be met regardless.

The following is a series of questions you can ask. These can be applied to writing and editing your writing:

Is your idea/argument a good or bad one?

Is my argument valid and defensible? Is it the opposite?

We have talked about how to determine whether an argument is valid, but you also need to defend your argument with premises and supporting details. If you cannot do this, your perspective will be easy to poke holes in and collapse like a house of cards.

The reason is something we have already talked about quite a bit. It is crucial because it will justify your position.

Stereotypes are not foolproof; therefore, they should not be used in an argument because there are many instances where they will not be valid. The same goes for clichés. Clichés are overused and only occur in a perfect situation.

Do I touch more profound points, or do I only scrape the surface when talking about my topic?

Go into detail! Details are so important, and the better support you have for your argument, the better. Don't be repetitive, but present as many different details as possible, especially in the first draft of your writing. You should strive to understand what you are writing about and encourage your readers to understand what they are reading.

Do I address the other points of view adequately?

Always consider the counterarguments. These will test your own viewpoint, and those who support the counterarguments will be looking for things that will take your argument down.

Do I question my ideas and test them for validity?

Question all of the evidence you find and make sure things like experiments and observation support it. If there are surveys involved in your argument, make sure the pool of people surveyed is an accurate proportion.

Create a goal and write it down. This will help you stick with the purpose of your argument.

When forming an argument and writing about it, you will need to give yourself time and be very organized. Your first step should be to research. Utilize all outlets that you have access to. Go to the library and read as much as you can about your topic first and write down important points and supporting details. Then, if you have access to any online databases, use those. Generally, depending on your topic, you will find statistics and experiments. Do not disregard anything because it does not directly address your viewpoint. Anything you can learn is good. The more you broaden your knowledge on the topic, the easier it will be for you to argue one way or another. You never know – halfway through, you may discover that you think the opposing viewpoint is better. Once you have searched databases, go to the search engines, and you will find the opinions of others and some more supporting details. The more information that you have and know about a topic, the easier your thoughts will flow. At this point, you should have several more sources than what is required. In the end, you will have to cut down the number of sources because you should not need them all.

Next, you should make outlines. That's right, multiple. Each should get more detailed, and by the end, you will have a sentence outline. This is essentially your first draft with different numbers and sections. You may think that making multiple outlines is excessive, but it will allow you to see your information in several different ways. When you look at the information in the same font in block paragraphs, it is difficult to determine whether it will be apparent to readers. This is why having someone else edit it is essential. Furthermore, if you don't have someone else, as long as you have given yourself enough time, you can put the project away and look at it the next day.

Your writing should not be confusing or full of hidden meaning. Make it as straightforward as possible. When you go through and edit, you should determine whether the following questions are easily found:

Is the purpose of the piece clear and easily found?

Stating the purpose in the first paragraph is the easiest way to do this. You are not trying to conceal your topic. There is no harm in including it in some of your first thoughts.

What questions does this piece answer? What questions are explored?

From what perspective is my argument?

You should know this for a couple of different reasons. Understanding your perspective will allow you to write about it clearer. It will also allow you to determine the opposing viewpoints and determine counterarguments.

Where did I get my information? Are the sources valid? Was the information consistent in all of my sources?

What concepts are central in my line of thinking?

These would be your main points, a standard number of main points is three, but you can have any number of main points to support your argument. These main points will have supporting details. They can be considered the premises of your arguments.

What conclusions am I making? What premises do I include?

These, of course, would be your entire argument. If you use a thesis statement, which you should, your premises and conclusions will be found here. Your thesis statement will only feature your premises and your conclusion. Write the premises in the order that they will appear to make the thesis statement more usable.

Am I making any assumption/s? Are these assumptions that I should be making?

There is a difference between making an educated inference and just making assumptions. For example, if there are no clouds in the sky, we can assume it will not rain. However, just because George Clooney is not your father does not mean you can assume he is your best friend's father. You must have evidence to support this.

As a writer who writes critically, you should be able to evaluate your work thoroughly. The questions above will help you with this. While you write, you will use several different thinking levels: validity, context, accuracy, and precision. The conclusions you make should be predictable when paired with all of the evidence you gathered. Always keep your argument reasonable, stable, and valid. Besides, you should always consider any weaknesses your argument has, along with potential counterarguments. How does considering counterarguments help you? Well, you will be able to strengthen your argument by pointing out the weaknesses in the counterarguments. You can also block the holes in your argument by strategizing and using critical thinking. Make your weaknesses seem like strengths in an argument.

Writing is essential and can help you think critically successfully. Writing requires you to do two things: write out your thoughts entirely and make them readable to a varied audience. Thinking critically is like speaking proper English to someone who learned it as a second language. You may be introducing a concept entirely new for your audience. This requires you to be extremely thorough, and you must know your topic thoroughly. Your awareness of a topic will increase when you write it out, and complex

problems can be worked through and solved.

Chapter 14:   Creative Thinking

Creativity is not solely about being an artist. Product managers need to be creative just as much as musicians, ballet dancers, or sculptors. Creative thinking is a crucial skill for all product managers to succeed in today's dynamic, complex, and interdependent global business environment (Gundry et al., 2016). Creating new products, developing countermeasures to problems, planning research projects, improving processes, and creating product education workshops require creative thinking skills. Generating and implementing new ideas is critical to the organization's success or failure (Bergendahl & Magnussion, 2015). Due to today's business environment's complexity and volatility, it is critical to continually develop new ideas (Sinfield et al., 2014).

Most people greatly underuse creativity based on society's conditioning processes, educational systems, and business organizations (Nolan, 1989). Most adults feel they are not creative; however, their creative abilities have just atrophied – they are not lost. Learning creative thinking tools and techniques, practicing, and creating an environment where critical judgment is suspended, and speculation encouraged to form the foundation for creating innovative products, services, and processes.

You need to become skilled at developing new ideas and any place, then putting those ideas into practice to develop innovative solutions. Search for new possibilities and actively use the information around you (de Bono, 1992). Explore new ways of thinking and challenge firmly held assumptions (Zaltman et al., 1982). Most importantly, discover and exploit opportunities to create competitive advantages and innovative solutions; do not wait for opportunities to appear (Gundry et al., 2016). Creative thinking aims to develop new and better ways to do things (de Bono, 1992).

When developing new ideas, focus on "what could be" and "what if" rather than "what is." Challenge tradition and current concepts and not be afraid of being wrong (de Bono, 1992). Ignore "killer phrases," which stifle creativity; for example, "It won't work," "We tried that before," or "It's not practical" (Biech, 1996). Do not allow the status quo to handcuff you and suppress creativity (Brandt & Eagleman, 2017). Not innovating is the most significant risk to poor performance (never doing anything new or never seeking alternatives) (Nolan, 1989).

Move beyond necessary business housekeeping activities (e.g., cutting costs, improving quality, enhancing customer service) and develop new ideas to drive future growth (de Bono, 1992). Focus on areas with no apparent problems and identify ways to improve these "perfect" areas (de Bono, 1992). Break things that are working fine. Focus on areas that you are not interested in or that because you discomfort; face challenges head-on and continually improve (Trott, 2015).

Create new ideas individually and then develop the ideas collectively with a cross-functional team (Carucci, 2017). Research has shown individual ideation to result in a higher quantity of quality, practical, and useable ideas than group ideation (Schirr, 2012). The goal of creative thinking is to create many ideas (divergent thinking). It is not about judging ideas: you do that during critical thinking (convergent thinking).

Do not try to develop new ideas ad hoc, or you will be wasting time – the most effective way to develop new ideas is with a deliberate, structured, and systematic process. Using a systematic process for creativity may sound counterintuitive; however, research has shown that participants developed a higher number of ideas when using a systematic process than ad hoc methods (Schirr, 2012).

James Webb Young (1960) identified a five-step creative process to develop new ideas.

1. Gather materials

2. Digest the information

3. Ignore the information – let it incubate (e.g., go for a walk, go to a movie)

4. An idea will appear out of nowhere

5. Apply the idea to the real world

Graham Wallas (2014) identified a similar process.

1. Preparation

2. Incubation

3. Illumination

4. Verification

Young and Wallas both noted that new ideas are typically combinations of many unrelated items. Developing creative ideas requires you to "connect the dots" from many different sources and experiences, aligning and combining unrelated areas. As your ideas incubate in your unconscious mind, the ideas expand and elaborate until a creative breakthrough emerges (Morris, 1992).

Most "new ideas" are the reconstruction of things you already know or have experienced. For example, smartphones combine the telephone, camera, internet, and voice recorder into a straightforward device. The snowmobile is a combination of a tractor, motorcycle, and snow skis. Continually exploring various subjects and exposing yourself to new experiences is critical to connecting unrelated "dots" to create new innovative ideas. Connecting disparate areas of study provides an endless supply of ingredients for new ideas. When you ask questions, experience new things, and develop a thorough understanding of the topic, you will create new ideas and develop innovative solutions to develop new opportunities.

The challenge of creative thinking is balancing structure and flexibility, divergent and convergent thinking, individual and group ideation, productivity and creativity, and art and science (Carucci, 2017). It is about overcoming mental blocks such as there is only one right answer, the idea is not logical, or you have to follow the rules (Jorgenson, 2018). You must work hard to overcome society's rigid, rule-driven, constraining systems (Ackoff & Rovin, 2005).

Creative thinking is exploring new ideas and exploiting existing ideas. It is difficult to get people out of their comfort zones and to move beyond the status quo (old habits die hard); however, for continued growth, you must become comfortable developing new ideas and challenging long-held beliefs – you must become comfortable with being uncomfortable. Adapt to change and reimagine the world (Brandt & Eagleman, 2007). Most importantly, do not overanalyze or judge your new ideas. Also, do not dismiss or abandon a new idea until you have given it sufficient time to develop.

Definitions

Four critical terms in creative thinking are imagination, creativity, innovation, and invention.

Creativity is developing new ideas: coming up with something new and original (Jorgenson, 2018). It is applied imagination: taking your wild thoughts and developing new ideas (Robinson, 2017). It is a continuous process of discovering and solving problems. Creativity is the capacity to find new and unexpected connections and find new relationships: a mindset that anything is possible (Prince, 2012). Mindlessly following rules does not lead to creativity. Creativity is about challenging or denying assumptions that constrain you from achieving what you want to accomplish (Ackoff & Rovin, 2005).

Good ideas are a dime a dozen. It is only after a new idea is translated into a reality that it becomes valuable: an innovation (Nolan, 1989). Innovation is the procedure of implementing creative ideas and introducing something new (Robinson, 2017). It is figuring out how to take a new idea and turn it into a product or service (Jorgenson, 2018).

The invention is creating something new that has never been developed. Merriam-Webster's online dictionary (2019) defines an invention as "to produce (something, such as a useful device or process) for the first time through the use of the imaginings or ingenious thinking and experiment."

New and improved ideas are the foundation for future success. Building the skills to develop new ideas any time and any place is critical for developing new products, devising effective marketing campaigns, or planning new product launches to confuse and surprise your competitors. An organization focused on continuous improvement will continuously be on the lookout for opportunities where new ideas can transform the business.

Society

People are creative, constructive, and exploratory beings, so why does creativity seem so difficult (Norman, 2013)? Why don't more people develop great new ideas? Unfortunately, creativity is often discouraged by our educational systems and business organizations. Also, society values adult practicality, consistency, and rigidity, diminishing our creative abilities and the desire to look beyond the obvious for alternative answers (Prince, 2012). Society values logic and judgment over imagination. As we mature, we undergo a conditioning process that suppresses our creativity (Basadur, 1995). Childhood playfulness is discouraged as we grow older and become engaged with traditional society.

Most of our creative skills atrophy due to societal influences, attitudes, behaviors, and thought processes (Basadur, 1995). The educational system is the leading cause of the lack of creativity in adults and organizations. Informal education, we learn what's acceptable and what's not (von Oech, 1998). Teachers typically have an expected, acceptable answer for questions or problems (Ackoff & Rovin, 2005). We are taught how to solve problems rather than look for opportunities. Throughout our schooling, we are taught to find the right answer, not to look for alternatives. Children are continually taught limitations instead of searching for many different options (Prince, 2012). It is essential to challenge the establishment and "color outside the lines continually."

The educational system also awards students for following the rules, rather than developing many new ideas and thinking originally (von Oech, 1998). Rules and the insistence on conformity puts a chokehold on children's innate, natural curiosity (Ackoff & Rovin, 2005). As adults, we too often accept workplace norms without question. Yes, it is essential to follow a variety of rules to survive in society (e.g., do not scream "fire" in a public place, stop at a red traffic light, raise your hand when wanting to speak); however, if you never challenge the rules or discard your "sacred cows" you will never be able to see the benefits of alternative ideas (von Oech, 1998).

There are benefits to conforming to societal norms, for example, cooperating with others and learning by observing how others react (von Oech, 1998). However, you need to challenge the status quo and live with a revolutionary mindset to create innovative products and services. You need courage, confidence, and persistence to achieve your dreams (Ackoff & Rovin, 2005).

Another reason for lack of creativity is that most people haven't been taught how to develop new ideas. Most people use ad hoc methods when new ideas are needed. However, creative thinking is a skill, and like other skills such as ice skating, cooking, or singing, it is developed by learning the basics and then practicing. Unfortunately, the majority of schools never teach structured methods for ideation. Most people struggle through life, trying to "think up" new ideas.

Finally, your own beliefs may prevent you from seeking new ideas (von Oech, 1998). Your schooling, religion, and community influence how you think and perceive the world. These "mental blocks" prevent you from proactively changing routine or moving beyond what is familiar (von Oech, 1998). Creativity is a skill and mindset. Learn the tools and techniques and adopt a mindset that strives for seeking multiple perspectives and a large number of possible alternatives.

Chapter 15: 5 Points of Interest in Systems Thinking and How to Utilize It

Systems thinking is a unique method for dealing with your association. A run of the mill association utilizes a wide range of techniques to showcase an item, purchase stock, oversee client connections, thus substantially more.

While business directors and business people utilize this thinking style, it is likewise unobtrusively developing in ubiquity in fields like cybernetics, science, and others. Specialists take a systemic viewpoint when making sense of how strategies work and how they can be increasingly proactive inside them.

As the following scarcely any decades unfurl, this type of thinking will turn out to be progressively significant. Supervisors should be skillful in comprehension and utilizing the standards behind this creative thinking style inside a worldwide domain.

The idea of system thinking is one of a kind method for drawing nearer methodic or systemic conduct. Fundamentally, it is an alternate method for seeing and discussing the truth we live in every day. By comprehension and thinking right now, likewise ready to make an alternative arrangement of tools for moving toward every issue.

At last, the objective is to comprehend the conduct of a necessary procedure. This, this way, permits you to make sense of how to oversee them.

A system is an assortment of interrelated or related parts at a basic level, which structure a brought together entirety. These interfacing parts need to cooperate, or they wouldn't be a piece of a system in any case.

For instance, an assortment of cushions on your bed isn't a system since they don't interface. On account of how the growths and form develop on the wood chips and feed creepy crawlies in the zone, this heap of chips would be an incredible case of a system in nature. Systems thinking adopt a comprehensive strategy to how various pieces of a procedure interrelate. In the customary investigation, individuals just took a gander at the different components in a system. By thinking in operations, you can comprehend the adjusting and fortifying procedures which cause system conduct.

A fortifying procedure is conduct that can prompt the system's breakdown whenever left unchecked by an adjusting procedure. This sort of behavior fundamentally builds a system part. Then, an adjusting procedure attempts to keep up the system's balance.

With this kind of thinking, it is critical to focus on the input you get. You might need to add laborers to a venture that is running bogged down for the executive's systems. As a general rule, including laborers may have hindered past undertakings since you needed to prepare approaching colleagues.

Rather than squandering assets, you'd search out an elective strategy. You may take a stab at evacuating a couple of steps simultaneously, booking more hours, or some other method to achieve the work on schedule.

With systems thinking, you can utilize outlines, charts, and PC reproductions to delineate and show systems conduct. At that point, this data permits you to foresee what will occur. The whole establishment of this thinking style started in 1956 with Educator Jay Forrester at the Massachusetts Organization of Innovation. While there are numerous tools for taking a gander at a system, conduct after some time (BOT) chart and a causal circle outline (CLD) are two of the most widely recognized. The CLD shows connections between various components in the system. In the examination, the BOT shows the activities of one or numerous factors over a set measure of time.

For directors, a reenactment model and an administration pilot test program are precious. The reenactment model permits you to take a gander at the collaboration of various components after some time. At that point, the administration pilot training program causes you to reenact how unique administration choices will influence the system.

Systems Way to deal with The executives

When you use system thinking in the executives and tasks, it causes you to settle on the correct business choices. Primarily, you investigate every business choice as per the systematic results it could have. On the off coincidental that you needed to purchase another assembling instrument, this sort of thinking would cause you to break down the expense of representative preparation, framework, and business postpone required.

Finally, the objective of thinking in systems is to assist you with evading sat around idly, cash, and different assets. A system's way to deal with the board thinks about the association as many interrelated and dynamic parts. Every one of these parts is a division and a sub-system inside your association.

Inside these divisions, there are significantly more subsystems. For the more prominent association to arrive at its objectives, these subsystems must have successful, ceaseless connections. It is these commonly needy parts and subparts cooperating, which make the entire association work appropriately.

The system approach includes coordinating objectives from various pieces of the association into the entire association. This permits the system to keep up parity and harmony. The system should likewise consolidate its objectives if it anticipates development.

This sort of thinking likewise takes a gander at the effect of present and future exercises. Associations must change because of inside and outside variables. In a perfect world, the association will likewise be a market chief as it makes a severe domain.

The system regularly includes various fields of study like brain science, promotion, bookkeeping, financial matters, and data systems in a business situation. By utilizing these fields of study adequately, the business can improve communications between various parts. From a systems perspective, the association can outline strategies, work in a social domain, and advance business goals effectively.

The 5 Focal points of Systems Thinking

While there are numerous focal points to the systems viewpoint in business, there are likewise a few downsides. Pundits accept this is just a hypothetical methodology, and it is difficult to characterize the specific connection between various segments in a genuine association.

Probably the most significant disadvantage is how explicit a systems approach is. It is inconceivable for the equivalent careful system to exist in various associations and offices. The systems approach doesn't offer a uniform idea that can work for a wide range of associations along these lines.

By using this methodology, you can make your work environment progressively productive and take an all-encompassing perspective. This methodology may also have the option to set aside your organization's cash over the long haul by improving your staffing needs and business activities.

1. Disappointment Can Be Something to Be Thankful For

One ordinary disclosure system scholars make about frustration. At the point when you see everything as a system, you aren't a disappointment. It is just the system that flopped briefly, not you or your association.

While you, at last, need your business to turn into a triumph, a few disappointments can be beneficial things that encourage exercises and lead to address choices being made later on. If Thomas Edison surrendered after making 9,999 bombed creations, he would have never succeeded. Instead, he broadly continued painful and discovered accomplishment after the next endeavor.

2. Advancement Is Critical

How are you going to build up a fruitful organization? What will you do to improve your representatives' work forms? Does it appear as though you are coming up short on approaches to beat your rivals?

You should comprehend the whole system to make changes to streamline the means in question. By utilizing a systems point of view, you can expel superfluous advances and find successful, accessible routes that can set aside your organization's cash.

3. A 3D Point of View

When you work in a particular office, you will, in general, observe answers for issues in your specific manner. A craftsman searches for a nail to fix a problem, and a bookkeeper goes after their number cruncher. As a business supervisor, you would prefer not to have such a limited, division explicit spotlight on settling issues as they will once in a while need similar endeavors to explain them.

Instead, you have to make a stride back and take a gander at the whole ecosystem and increase a transdisciplinary comprehension of the system.

This all-encompassing perspective causes you to open your imagination and find better approaches to accomplish your hierarchical objectives.

4. Find Interconnectivity

There are work environments where individuals from various offices continually chance upon one another. The architects made these structures to increment interdepartmental correspondences and cause good fortune, which prompts unordinary arrangements.

With a systems approach, you understand everything is progressively interrelated. Every individual needs their colleagues to make progress.

5. Building Up an Adoration for Issues

More often than not, chiefs effectively work to maintain a strategic distance from issues. While you ought to likely limit adverse difficulties or problems with collaboration among your gathering, a few issues merit seeking after additional detail. Taking care of a complicated issue could give you a superior method for leading business, another creation of an altogether extraordinary way to deal with life.

Rather than staying away from multifaceted nature, a systems approach causes you to consider issues to be energizing chances. These issues offer potential strategies to enhance and build up your inventiveness. As opposed to avoiding troublesome issues, your workers transform into dynamic issue solvers.

Receiving a Systems Approach in Your Work environment

Regardless of how huge or little your association is, it, without a doubt, incorporates various systems that cooperate to accomplish your targets at the point when you just location one piece of the issue, you will probably never locate a long haul arrangement. By taking a gander at the system's interconnected elements, you can find a superior method for directing your business.

Systems thinking can assist you with upsetting your working environment over each vertical. On the off chance that you set the systems way to deal with work in your organization, a superior and progressively active business could be directly around the bend.

Chapter 16:   Clear Thinking

How to Think Clearly

Check Your Attitude

Your ability to think clearly will largely depend on your desires. Often, you will find it easy to sit down and think of the strategies you can adopt to achieve your goals. Of course, this is dependent on if you have goals. When you don't want to achieve something, it is also easy to think of all the things you can do to accomplish this. Therefore, to think clearly, it is imperative, to be honest about your goals and ambitions. Is this something that you want in your life? Ideally, developing the right attitude will help bring clarity to the goals that you wish to attain.

Use Your Passion

There is a good reason why successful people will always advise you to follow your passion. The reality is that you have never heard them tell you to follow your emotions. Your passion for a particular goal will help you to overcome any challenges associated with it. Passion drains away all the negative thoughts that could deter you from thinking clearly about the task ahead. Conversely, emotions will do just the opposite. Letting your emotions to get the best of you will make you feel overwhelmed about what you should do. Usually, you will find yourself focusing more on the obstacles that you must go through. Therefore, to think clearly, it is advisable to use passion to keep your emotions in check.

Use Negative Thinking

It might sound controversial that you should use negative thinking to help you. It is possible. Remember, we are talking about finding the right frameworks to help you understand something better. So, it is worthwhile to consider how negative thinking can help clear your mind.

Believe it or not, there is an optimistic power in negative thinking. When striving to achieve goals, most people will embrace the idea of thinking positively. Indeed, thinking positively works in many ways. It gives your mind a chance to focus your energy on what you can do to ensure you accomplish set goals. Therefore, looking at this from a positive perspective, you can take advantage of your negative thinking to bring about positivity.

Use Cool Logic

Achieving a clear focus, you need on what you want to achieve might be comfortable in the short run. Most people find it easy to concentrate for a few weeks or months before losing track of their doing. Therefore, to ensure that you maintain a clear focus on what you desire, you should use cool logic. How does this work? Cool logic relates to the idea of concentrating on the issue at hand. You should not allow anything else to distract you. For example, if you are working on a project, your mind should concentrate on the project and nothing else. Typically, it is easy to get distracted and allow your ego to control how you think. In this case, you will be withdrawn to think about how you are better than others in doing a particular task. As a result, instead of concentrating on the task at hand, you will pay too much attention to competing with your colleagues. Ultimately, this will hurt the outcome of the project.

Challenge Your Preferences

Several presumptive beliefs could affect the clarity of your thoughts. The ideas you have developed in your mind about a particular issue can deter you from thinking about anything else. Many people will want to settle for the most expensive wines simply because they believe in the notion that the price of the bottle determines how the wine tastes. However, this might not be true if you engage in a blind taste test. You might come across something that you will like. The point here is that you should challenge your preferences by trying something that you have never done before. You will be surprised that you could make informed decisions to the least of your expectations.

Think About Thinking

The aspect of being aware of your thought processes is termed metacognition. For you to think clearly, you should be aware of how you are thinking. Therefore, you shouldn't allow your thoughts to flow freely without being aware of them. Instead, you must plan and assess how you are thinking. The advantage gained through metacognition is that you will enrich your learning experience. For instance, your self-awareness will drive you to think clearly about how to accomplish a particular task.

Ideal Mental Models for Clear Thinking

First Principles Thinking

Some problems appear too complicated for us to solve. Without a doubt, this is a dilemma that most people go through in their lives. Well, you shouldn't be stuck when faced with such circumstances because you can apply mental models. An ideal mental model to use here would be the first principles of thinking. This model is highly recommended when dealing with challenging situations. The best part is that this framework will push you to think for yourself.

The first principles of thinking have been there for several years, but it recently became famous in 2002 after Elon Musk stressed the importance of using them. This framework focuses on the idea that one should think like a scientist. The reason for taking this direction is because scientists don't use assumptions. Their conclusions are often made after facts have been proven.

Theoretically, first principles thinking will require an individual to think critically about a particular situation until they are left with the truths that define the problem they are facing. This is to means that you shouldn't make decisions like other people. You should mull over thinking deeper. The easiest way of grasping this principle's meaning is that when faced with a problem, the primary thing that you should do is to deconstruct. After that, focus on reconstructing.

The first step of deconstructing requires asking yourself intelligent questions regarding your situation or problem at hand. Additionally, you should have a bottomless understanding of frameworks from distinct disciplines. You must get more information about varying forms of mental models. Your knowledge is required to guarantee that you can look at your problem from varying perspectives.

Your next move will be to bring together the pieces you had broken down in the first step. Again, for you to effectively reconstruct, you have to practice how to do it. You could have an idea of how to do something. However, a standalone idea cannot help you to make the right decisions.

You need to combine several ideas to make valid conclusions. Practicing this more often will strengthen your mental muscles. Eventually, you will improve your thinking skills and end up making sound decisions.

Thought Experiment

The thought experiment mental model can help you think clearly by solving difficult problems. The thought experiment encourages speculation. What's more, it forces people to alter their paradigms. Instead of reasoning like other people, the thought experiment model pushes you out of your comfort zone. As a result, it forces you to ask yourself rhetorical questions that are complex. This style of thinking unveils the things that you don't know and some of which you know.

The advantage of using the thought experiment is that it encourages innovative ideas by pushing you beyond your thinking boundaries. Therefore, you will not be limited to the things that you already know. One major challenge with this mental model is that it appears impractical. Nevertheless, scholars believe that it can be used theoretically.

BATNA

BATNA is the acronym for Best Alternative to a Negotiated Agreement. This mental model can help you during negotiations. Typically, there are instances when negotiations reach a deadlock. This is a situation whereby parties cannot agree on a particular issue. In such cases, there should be an ideal alternative since the parties negotiating cannot agree.

It is worth noting that BATNA should be taken into consideration even before engaging in negotiations.

Compounding Knowledge

Compounding knowledge is a mental model rooted in the economic concept of compounding interest. It can be understood as the growth that emerges from your past growth. The framework is not only applicable in your investments, but it can also be applied to your business, relationships, and knowledge.

People are always on the verge of consuming information. What they fail to realize is that most of them consume expiring information. This is something that Warren Buffett strives to steer away from. Instead of focusing on consuming information that is not important, Buffett focuses on equipping himself with the knowledge to help him manage his companies successfully. The idea here is to learn something new that would positively change what you do.

Gaining and gathering information from time to time will undeniably lead to compounding benefits. Learning something today and combining it with something else that you learn on the following day will make you a better person. Filling your mind with expiring information that is of less importance is easy, but the reality is that it will not help you in days or months to come.

Occam's Razor

Occam's Razor is a mental model that is attributed to William of Ockham. He did not introduce the term, but his reasoning style inspired people to come up with the heuristic. The simplest way of comprehending this concept is that the simplest solution to a particular problem is correct.

We cannot deny the fact that we always strive to simplify our lives. Everybody does. However, we find ourselves complicating how we live and how we deal with our problems. Interestingly, some billionaires astound us with the way they choose to live their lives. Mark Zuckerberg is a good example. It is not uncommon to see him in a gray T-shirt. If you can recall, Steve Jobs also wore his black turtleneck on almost all occasions. This raises eyebrows, right? Indeed, these folks can afford fancy outfits, but they choose to wear similar outfits most of the time.

Using Occam's Razor philosophy, simplicity is the key to success. The idea of wearing similar clothes every day, as evidenced by some billionaires, is a way of saving themselves time. Without a doubt, knowing that you will wear a gray T-shirt every day can help you save time. Moreover, it can save you brainpower that you can use in making informed decisions. The point here is that you should not allow trivial things to distract you from focusing on what is essential.

Chapter 17:   What is Systems Thinking

Systems thinking is a holistic approach to research that focuses on how the parts of a system interrelate and how systems work overtime and within larger systems. Systems thinking approaches contrast with traditional research, which examines structures by breaking them down into their elements. Systems analysis can be used in any research area and has been applied, among many others, to studying medical, environmental, political, cultural, human resources, and educational systems.

System action stems from the consequences of cycles of reinforcement and adjustment according to system thought. A strengthening process leads to an increase in some parts of the system. If a balancing mechanism does not search for reinforcement, it eventually leads to failure. A mechanism of balance is one that seeks to maintain equilibrium in a given system.

What are the forces that strike—the forces that cause these unintended consequences? Systems thinking provides us with a clue. Systems thinking is a method of looking at the world as one big system made up of countless interconnected smaller systems. These parts can be linked via various positive, adverse, and nonlinear effects that can lead to unintended consequences.

What Does It Involve?

The word "systems thinking" can mean different things for people. It is essential to note. The discipline of system thought is more than a set of instruments and methods – it is also a theory that underlies it. Many beginners like causal loop charts and control flight simulators are drawn to technologies to expect these technologies to assist them in coping with persistent business problems. Structures thought, however, is also the sensitivity of the systemic existence of the environment in which we live; the understanding of the role of the process in creating the conditions we face; knowledge of the robust laws of structures which we do not understand.

Thinking technology is also a diagnostic tool. Like in the medical profession, accurate diagnosis accompanies successful treatment. In this sense, system thinking is a systematic method for a more thorough and reliable analysis of issues before acting. This helps us to ask informed questions before we conclude.

Systems analysis also requires shifting from events or data to behavioral overtime trends and processes underlying these trends and events. We will extend the options available, and create more meaningful, long-term solutions for chronic issues by identifying and modifying systems that are not well served (including our mental models and perceptions).

Generally, the viewpoint of systems thinking requires curiosity, insight, compassion, preference, and courage. This approach requires the ability to look at the situation in more detail, realize that we interconnect, realize that an issue often includes multiple solutions and championship approaches that might not be common.

When to Use?

Problems suitable for systems-oriented intervention have the following features:

- The problem is relevant.

- The problem is persistent, not one-off.

- The issue is well known, and its history is well known.

- People have tried to solve the problem unsuccessfully before.

How do we Use System Thinking Tools?

Diagrams of Causal Chain. Recall, first, that less is more. Start small and simple; add additional elements to the story if needed—present the plot. The number of elements in a loop will be dependent on the needs of the story and the individuals using the diagram. A concise explanation may be sufficient to encourage conversation and provide a new way of seeing a problem. In other cases, you can need more loops to explain causal relationships.

Keep in mind also that people always assume that a diagram will contain all possible variables in a story; this is not generally true. In other cases, external factors do not change, change very slowly, or are irrelevant to the problem. You can complicate things unnecessarily by sharing this information, especially those that you have little or no control over. Many of the most successful loops show links or interactions between parts of the organization or program that the community has not previously identified.

Ultimately, don't ask if a loop is "right." Ask yourself then if the loop correctly represents the narrative the community wants to tell. Loops are brief explanations of what we consider to be a current reality; they are "correct" enough to represent that viewpoint.

The Archetypes

Keep it general and straightforward when using archetypes or classical stories in systems thought. If the community wants to know more about an archetype, then you can go into more specifics.

Do not attempt to "sell" archetypes; once people see the similarities between archetypes and their problems for themselves, they will understand more. Nevertheless, you should seek to demystify the archetypes by connecting them to shared interactions that we all share.

Chapter 18:   Practice Systems Thinking

Your environment has an enormous impact on the way you feel and the actions you take. When your environment is working against you, it is challenging to adopt a positive mindset and take the actions required to achieve your goals. For example, if people are casting doubts about your ability to succeed, you'll find it difficult to believe in or work toward any dream.

Therefore, to design the reality you want, you must surround yourself with positive people who will bring the best out of you. You must also ensure your environment facilitates the new behaviors and habits you want to adopt.

Changing your peer group

It's said that we are the average of the five people we spend the most time with. Who are these five people for you? If you keep your current circle of friends, how likely are you to achieve your biggest dreams?

You'll tend to pick up the attitudes, habits, and ways of thinking of people around you. To a certain extent, we can say that people you hang out with dictate how you think, feel, and act. For this reason, you'll seldom—if ever—see successful people hanging out with negative or unsuccessful people any more than they have to.

Remember, whatever your goals or dreams, reaching them won't be easy. You'll need all the support you can gather, and this should start by surrounding yourself with the right people.

1. How to protect yourself from negative people

As you develop a new reality model to reach your goals, you'll encounter naysayers and other dream killers. Although it is expected, it doesn't mean you should permit them to influence your reality model. These people have their vision of the world, and that's fine, but don't let them get into your head, drag you down and mess with your dreams. Instead, strengthen your model of reality by improving your peer group and building rock-solid confidence in yourself and your vision.

The truth is, in any interaction between you and another person, two realities clash. If you lack confidence and conviction, you're more likely to be sucked into the other person's version of "reality." This means you will allow their model of reality (i.e., their assumptions) to influence yours. For instance, if you lack confidence and expect you to fail, it may lead you to reconsider your goals. If they say your art, book, or product sucks, you may decide to give up. On the other hand, if they believe in you and offer encouragement, you'll feel great about yourself and become more optimistic.

This is why you must learn to develop more confidence and distance yourself from negative people. Over time and as you gain confidence, you'll be less affected by other people's opinions. Even so, there is no reason to hang out with naysayers any longer than you have to, right?

Now let's look at a few steps you can take to deal more effectively with negative people. You can:

Ask for their support,

Reduce the time you spend with them, or

Refrain from sharing your goals with them.

a. Ask for their support

The first thing you can do is to ask them to support you. To do so, tell them precisely what you're trying to accomplish and why it's important to you. Tell them why their help is so important and how much it would mean for you to have their full support.

In a perfect world, your friends and family will support you and want the best for you, but that's not always the way things work. If you notice no change in their attitude after talking with unsupportive people in your life, try spending less time with them.

It's best not to spend all day around negative people. If you notice someone is dragging you down, take specific measures to distance yourself from that person. For instance, you can decide to meet him or her only once a week instead of two or three times a week. You can also decline invitations more often. By doing so, this toxic relationship may naturally die off over time.

Another step you can take to defend yourself from negative people is to avoid sharing your goals. If you feel they won't support you, just keep your goals for yourself and only share them with people who will encourage you. Repeatedly being told that you will fail with your new venture, never land your dream job or struggle to get your book published is a real downer. Cherish your dreams and only share them with people who deserve to know about those who have your best interests at heart.

Now, what about the people you live with? How should you deal with them? Here are a few tips you can try.

Ask for their input/advice. Ask them what they would do if they were in your shoes? For instance, how would they go about changing careers? What would they do if they needed to retire ten years early?

Further, include them in your dream. If your goal or dream is something you believe they can benefit from, sell them on it. But instead of persuading them yourself, ask them how their life would be better once you reach that goal. In short, let them sell themselves on your goal. For instance, let's say you want to retire early by saving aggressively and investing your money. Your partner might not be on board with your plan at first. However, you could ask them to imagine what they would be doing if they could retire earlier than sixty-five. You could ask what would excite them most about early retirement. Once they have straightforward and exciting goals themselves, they may change their mind about your idea and start helping you progress towards your goal.

Get early results. Another option is to generate tangible results to show to your spouse, kids, and parents. A couple of years ago, I received an email from one of my readers who loved my goal setting book and wanted his spouse to read it. However, she wasn't too keen on the idea. I suggested the best thing he could do was to start achieving goals, and as he did so, she might feel inspired and pick up the book, too. It's easier to change others by becoming a role model than by issuing instructions. Most people don't like to be told what to do.

If none of these suggestions work, you might have to pursue your goals without their support. If they're acting against your goal, you have two options—either give up on your goal or carry on regardless of the consequences it may have on your relationship.

d. Surround yourself with people who will support you

One of the most effective ways to change how you think, feel, and act is to change the people you hang out with. You need to be around positive and successful people who will push you to become your best self and demand more of you. Here are a few things you can do to be around such positive people:

Join groups of like-minded people.

Create your event.

Look for a mentor.

Hire a coach.

To strengthen your reality model, you need to surround yourself with people on the same path and, if possible, ahead of you. For instance, if you're an entrepreneur, you might want to join a group of entrepreneurs. If you are an aspiring writer, you might join Facebook groups dedicated to writers or attend author conferences.

Don't hesitate to contact people who are on the same path as you. The people who helped me the most are people I contacted myself. So be proactive. Even a few encounters can make a significant difference in your life.

What group or groups could you join? Who could you contact?

Create your event

If you can't find your tribe, why not create an event that will attract people you want to be surrounded with? For instance, last year, I created a mastermind group with two other authors. The group has allowed us to share tips and strategies and have helped us achieve better results.

What about you? Who do you want to attract into your life, and what kind of event could you organize to appeal to them?

Having a mentor is one of the most effective ways to skyrocket your success. A great mentor will:

Help you shift your mindset,

Tell you what to do (and not to do), saving you months or years of work,

Ask you smart questions and offer guidance, and

Open their network to you (potentially).

However, finding the right mentor can be challenging. The more successful a person is, the busier they are—and the harder it will be to reach them.

There is no magic way to find a mentor, but there are a few things you can do to help get you started. The most important thing is to put yourself in the shoes of a potential future mentor. You need to think as he or she thinks. For instance, if I were to mentor someone, the main question I would ask myself is how committed that potential mentee is. I don't want to waste my time with someone who will disappear in a few months.

The bottom line is; you must be a good asset for your mentor. Many prosperous people are happy to share their knowledge and wisdom, but they want to make sure it will be worth their time. Abide this in mind when you look for a teacher. If you work hard on yourself first and aim to add value to your mentor, maybe they will decide to work with you.

Don't worry if you can't find a mentor. You can always have virtual mentors by reading books, buying courses, or watching videos.

f. Hire a coach

Another way to find support and make tangible progress toward your goals is to work with a coach. By participating your hard-earned money in a coach, you'll also have skin in the game, making it more likely you'll take action and generate results.

Chapter 19: Systems Thinking towards Business Success

Systems thinking can provide a substantial edge in business and your career. And, in the world of business, any competitive advantage is valuable. What type of tangible effect might arise from systems thinking? Would finding unique and unanticipated solutions or products interest you? How about avoiding unproductive options or actions that may have damaging side effects? And how about your career? First, let's recognize a complex interplay between cooperation and competition between employees (something we will explore in great depth). Whenever there is more than one employee at a company, there is some allocation of limited resources (e.g., salary), and employees who have special skills are the most valuable.

You may think that college education, business training, and experience have prepared you for the situations you will face in business. Your experiences may well prepare you for 90% of the situations you are likely to face, but what about the other 10%? Although these exceptional experiences may occur infrequently, they could be disproportionately impactful and could be crucial turning points for your organization or career. In these cases, the systems methods can be of great benefit.

To illustrate systems thinking, let's explore an example.

To be a low-price carrier, People Express needed a low-cost structure. Salaries are a large component of costs, so People Express used an incentive-based salary structure. Management gave employees a low base salary along with stock incentives. If People Express stock did well, employees were very well compensated, even with a low base. This created the feedback loop, as shown in the figure. The low employee base salaries allowed People Express to charge low ticket prices while still delivering excellent customer service. These low prices allowed air travel to compete with other transportation businesses such as buses and trains. As consumers switched from buses to People Express flights, the total available market for airlines grew. In the early 1980s, People Express was the primary low-cost carrier and garnered most of this new traffic. That led to growth in People Express' revenue and margin. As People Express' revenue and the margin grew, their stock price increased. As the stock price increased, the employees cashed in their incentives and grew in enthusiasm correspondingly. This reinforcing feedback loop would be characterized as a virtuous feedback loop since the feedback loop's growth helps achieve the company's goals.

Businesses will need to hire employees who can think critically if they want to remain competitive and efficient. Hiring someone with a college degree is not enough. Curious, logical, and strong problem-solvers will have to be new hires. According to industry studies, when assessing job candidates, tactical and System Thinking is the capability most needed by businesses worldwide. Employers expect that recruits have more than knowledge of textbooks and technical skills and agree that System Thinking is crucial for job performance and career flexibility. It was also discovered that System Thinking was deemed the most essential attribute that would help their businesses grow, more than creativity or improved IT.

Job environments are rapidly shifting into new job positions pressuring workers. Right decisions include concentrating on the most relevant information, asking the right questions, and making the right conclusions that too few workers have these skills. In a study of Human Resource Managers (SHRM), it was discovered that a full 70 percent of high school workers lost System Thinking skills. In other recent studies, during the first two years of college, forty-five percent of college graduates made no noticeable improvement in the development of System Thinking or reasoning skills. Thirty-six percent did not show any significant gains in System Thinking skills after four years. When these students leave college and enter the workforce, they will not be prepared to meet the working world's challenges. If managers say System Thinking skills are highly valued, candidates exhibiting these skills will be in demand and rare to find. The skills of System Thinking will become invaluable. Certain types of jobs and work environments change. Flexibility and adaptability will become crucial to meeting real-world conditions and will need to be screened for in interviews by human resources professionals and recruiters. It will also become essential to develop the System Thinking skill sets of your existing employees.

One approach for professionals with human resources is to use preliminary hiring thinking assessments. Individuals who score well on these tests display good analytical skills, judgment, decision-making, and performance overall. They often demonstrate the ability to assess the given data's value, are innovative, have better job skills, and often move up in your company. There are some evaluations for managerial or professional candidates evaluating hard skills. Research also demonstrates that higher-level management positions require System Thinking skills and the ability to learn and accurately process information quickly. Organizations that include both System Thinking and personality testing in hiring practices will have a greater overall candidate perspective than organizations that use personality or System Thinking evaluations alone.

Through incorporating probing strategies, it is possible to help workers become tactical thinkers and higher-order thinkers. Better interviewing allows the learner to more efficiently interpret and synthesize data. The method can become automated by repetition to transfer information in new situations and scenarios. Some classes teach students not great thinkers or questioners to be good listeners. Passive thinking does not automatically improve cognitive skills or behavioral changes. It will be more successful in participating actively in the learning process and will deliver more long-term outcomes.

Knowledge gained and interpreted by thinking of the higher-order is stored longer than conventional memorization. Knowledge is more comfortable to transfer and implement, resulting in a better solution to problems. Then the questioning becomes a vital part of the process of teaching and learning. Perfecting the questioning art begins with determining what is known and allows the instructor or mentor to develop new ideas and understandings. It is possible to use probing methods to promote students' ability to think. Create relevant questions. Focus on the technique you use. Encourage interactive discussion and promote engagement.

Open-ended questions usually lead the student to analyze and evaluate more effectively. A skilled questioner's most essential elements are asking short and concise questions, rephrasing, and drawing additional answers from the student's answers. There is also a need for training to learn every skill. Offer your group the opportunity to practice the ideas, talents, behaviors, and behavioral changes that come from your questions, and choose appropriate experiences that enable them to learn. Find a scenario that draws on what they already learn when dreaming about circumstances to add a new employee or mentee. Then model an issue that shows the correct process of thinking. Propose a dilemma that can be overcome by working together or talking through the situation. Also, for exploratory questions, use your inquiry strategy. What would you do if that happened? Explain what happened to me? What are we going to do? Perhaps there's a discussion. What's going to happen next? Finally, provide some form of input and create a chance for self-assessment. Use this feedback to build on your next lesson and never forget creative thinking to be rewarded. If they don't feel it is valued, the learners won't want to repeat their behavior.

You will know that when the problem is visualized and can be described and explained, there is higher-order thinking. The learner will also differentiate between relevant and non-relevant information and search for reasons why something is happening or the root cause. They will rationalize or explain why a solution will work and see different angles or sides of a problem. Try to draw on challenges in the real world. This not only lets the student use the data in the correct reference frame, but it also allows you to solve problems in your company or business in the real world. Encourage your learner to think about the strategies you are introducing, as this will reinforce that this is a valuable process to implement when solving problems repeatedly. Suppose recruiters and managers begin to look for employees with these skills and use the art of questioning for existing employees. In that case, System Thinking will become invaluable to the future success of your organization. There is a competitive advantage for businesses that can recruit and grow System Thinkers. With these capabilities, too few workers are employed, with few finding chances to improve them.

Chapter 20: Steps to Changing the Way You Think

The thing about procrastination and laziness is that it all comes down to your mindset. I'd go so far as saying the state of affairs in your life right now reflects what your state of mind has been. If you don't like it, the first step is not to change what you've been doing but to change your state of mind. When you transition to the state of mind that your ideal version of yourself would have, then taking the actions needed to be more productive becomes more comfortable, and everything you do to achieve that is a lot more effective.

A Negative Mindset

When you decide to do something, it can be hard to stick with it. This is especially the case where it's something that ultimately falls to you and no one else. In times like this, it's easy to get cynical. If you let your mindset become a negative one, then you will find that you're continually moving from bad situations to even worse ones. You can't focus. You can't think creatively. You have the energy for nada, and so nada is what you do. So, what are these negative mindsets that hold you back from achieving your most significant potential?

Feelings of inadequacy. If you find that you're always beating up on yourself, no matter how many clients you've made happy or how much effort you have put into your projects, then you have the wrong mindset. You can't expect to be a winner in life when deep down inside, you feel like you keep losing, and you'll never be good enough.

The fix: Do you feel like you are good enough. A great way to do this is to look back on Forgoing successful ventures so that you can feel confident about your abilities. Don't just look back, though. Look ahead as well. Don't settle and assume that your current output is all you're capable of. Know that there's always room for improvement. When you become lackadaisical about your work, your colleagues, bosses, and clients will notice. They, too, will become that way to you, and you become dispensable.

Feelings of hopelessness. In life, you've just got to have some metal for you. Otherwise, you will find that you're always defeated before you even start the game. Or, if you have one little mistake or failure, you just throw up your hands and quit. You need to change right away.

The fix: Don't be too quick to accept defeat. Also, make peace with failures and mistakes. There's nothing wrong with failing because it's all part of the process of success. Suck it up, knowing that mistakes always teach you more, and failures help you get better. Don't let them chip away at your drive.

Impatience and desperation. This is not a good vibe at all, in any aspect of life. Do you find that you're always impatient with the pace at which your work is going? Are you frustrated because things are not happening as quickly as you'd like? Well, then you'd better watch out! This feeling of impatience can lead to you making some terrible choices that will not work out fine for you in the long run. It could hurt your project or whatever business it is you're running.

The fix: Recognize that good thing take time. Sure, sometimes, what you want can happen fast. However, learn to be like a patient crocodile, waiting for its prey to swim to it before it snaps its jaws shut. Only ever make decisions and act when you're feeling stable and in no rush.

Feelings of helplessness. When you start something new, you are the one who is responsible for whether it flies or dies. You might think this responsibility is a bit much for you to bear, and as such, you're overwhelmed by feelings of helplessness. Don't be.

The fix: Recognize that just like riding a bike, these are things that will feel natural to you over time; don't sweat it too much. Think back to all the times you started something new and were uncertain, yet were able to make it work. This new project or business you've got going is no different from those times.

Overwhelmed by fear. The thing about fear is that you're choosing to believe in a terrible turn of events that is not real. It has not played out yet. If you find that you're always giving in to your fearful thoughts, then you're either going to be completely paralyzed and unable to move forward with your goals, or you'll be taking all the wrong decisions from a place of fear.

The fix: Understand the worst that could happen, and then gently remind yourself that it would not be the end of the world. Then go ahead and do whatever it is you need to be more productive.

Shame. Shame can be a terrible thing when you choose to wallow in it. When you make mistakes, do you find yourself continually rehashing them in your head, to the point where you can't even think of a way forward? Then you must change that mindset.

The fix: Understand that crap happens. Get over it. There's no such thing as perfect, and you'll never be it. Focus on the way forward, rather than wallowing in the past.

Underwhelm. Do you find that you're ultimately unsatisfied with the quality of your work? Are you bored, perhaps? Do you wonder every so often if you're even in the right field? Feelings of dissatisfaction plague you. Sometimes, what you do may feel underwhelming. There's no challenge. If all your neurons except two went on vacation, you'd be able to do what you do efficiently. You don't feel like you're growing at all. You hate it, but you've grown comfortable. It's time to shake things up.

If you're always dragging your feet in the morning or looking for any chance to hop on to something new because it's a lot more fun than what you've been doing, then you're due for a mental tune-up.

The fix: Know that you always have the option to make changes. You don't have to stay stuck where you are. As that profound saying goes, "Move. You are not a tree." Even trees spread out their roots and branches! Get a picture of what your dream day would be like, and then make plans and take action to make it happen.

Overwhelm. This is a common one, especially when you're self-employed. You might feel like you have an impossible workload. You feel like you're completely out of control and continuously having to dance to other people's tunes.

The fix: Recognize your signs of burnout. Be willing to admit that you may have pushed a little too hard, and you require a break. Also, be honest with yourself about whether you're adequately compensated, and then work towards fixing that.

Other mindsets that don't work for you feel like you're unproductive, disorganized, and must do things on your own instead of the delegate. Feelings of being broke, resentful, guilty, and alone also do not help in any way at all. So how do you change your mindset, exactly?

Chapter 21:   The Systems View

Step 1:

The systems thinking experts started unwinding the problem backward. There were no denying Acme's sales were decreasing by the day and that potentially new and current customers were choosing Acme's competitors as a supplier.

Step 2:

Based on what was identified in Step 1, known as the critical problem, systems thinking experts started digging deeper. What was the most direct reason for the drop in sales?

They concluded that Acme's poor service (the flawed billing and delivery delays) was the direct reason for customer loss. The direct reason was not hard to guess as these symptoms were the most visible. But what about the indirect reasons behind the poor service?

Step 3:

What was causing poor service?

After spending time with Acme employees and talking about their work routines, it turned out the employees were overwhelmed by "special orders." The amount of regular automated orders had decreased while the amount of these special orders had dramatically increased. Since the billing requirements were also unique, the chances of billing errors also increased and were the cause of the billing issues. The responsibilities and tasks of the employees had grown, but the number of employees had not. All these stressful factors' cumulated effect put an increased burden on the service department employees, which resulted in poor service and then resulted in a drop in sales.

Step 4:

Step 3 revealed a new, ignored, problematic element in the Acme equation: the special orders. Where were the special orders coming from?

The systems thinking professionals needed the answer to this question, so they turned to the sales manager. Following the interview, it turned out the manager, to counterbalance the market's hazards and supply sufficiently attractive product packages, had come up with creative and unique packages to increase sales. He'd congratulated his team's efforts, noting the special pricing and expanded delivery options were both attractive features for new customers.

Step 5:

The sales manager failed to notice how these new "attractive" features were sabotaging, rather than helping, the company's overall success. The manager admitted the main reason for coming up with new features was the desperate need to find new customers to keep Acme's sales on track.

And thus, the loop closed for Acme. Remember where we started in Step 1? Acme's main problem was customer loss.

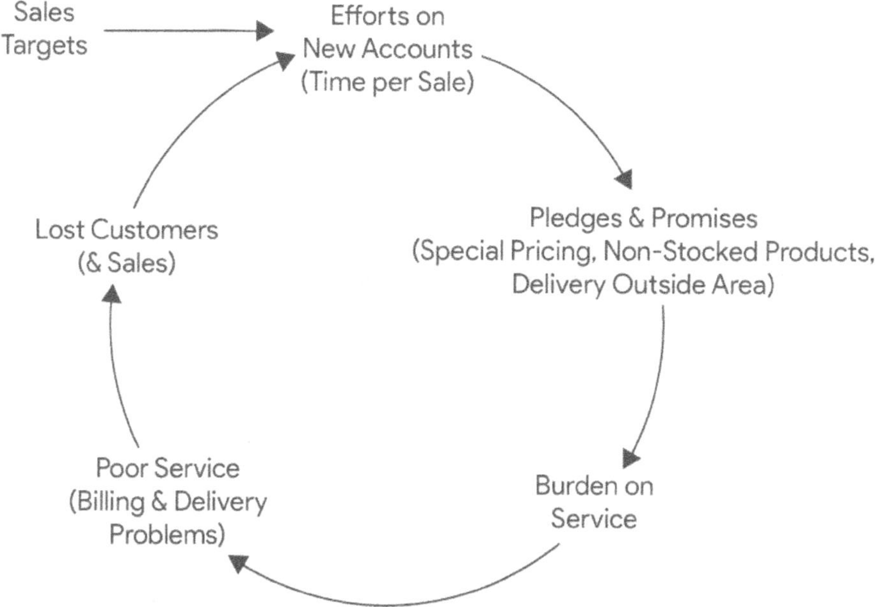

If you read counter-clockwise, starting from "lost customers," you'll see

the deductive logic systems thinking experts used to dig deeper and get to

the bottom of Acme, Inc.'s issues. Now start reading clockwise from "sales

targets." To meet sales targets, the sales department needed to bring in new

customers. How could they do that? By outperforming other competitors

in the form of special features. They dumped their innovations onto an

unprepared and already busy service department, which caused an even

greater division of their attention. Their frustration and lack of

computerized systems led to human errors and, in the grand scheme of

things, poor service drove customers away. What did Acme do in response to this? The sales department saw the poor sales numbers, so they put more effort into overly complicated special packages and caused even more burden on the service employees.

In systems thinking, we call this phenomenon reinforcing feedback, meaning the actions taken reinforced whatever was already going on in the loop.

Before we move on with the story of Acme, Inc., let's take a closer look at how the systems thinking team analyzed the problem differently than the first consulting team.

The original consulting team had focused on the most visible symptoms, considering each point independently from one another. On the other hand, the systems thinking team dug deeper into the problem, starting from the most visible.

The systems thinking view also shed light on the lack of communication between departments (in this case, the sales and service departments) and had them work on solutions together instead of independently trying to fix each department's issues. The consulting team focused on each part of Acme separately. Simultaneously, the systems thinking experts took a holistic, big-picture view of the company's product mismanagement and then went a level lower to investigate the role of different departments. Even when they discovered the cause of the problem, the system thinking experts did not separate the two departments involved but instead encouraged a solution through communication and cooperation.

True enough, before we start casting aspersions toward the consultation company, let's take a moment to think about our approaches to solving problems in our own lives. Be honest with yourself and answer these questions:

• Do I usually approach my problems with a linear or systemic solution?

• Why don't I choose to use the systemic approach more often?

I would assume your answer to the first question to be a "linear solution" rather than a systemic approach. Most of us think this way, and for a good reason. The majority of our everyday problems don't require deep systemic analysis. If your watch stops, you change the battery. If you're hungry, you eat. If you miss your mom, you call or visit her. If it rains, you grab your umbrella. I could go on with the list of mundane problems that would make us go nuts if we attempted to solve with a systemic view. There are, however, some problems in our lives that can't be fixed with a simple "if this then that" approach. These are the real problems, the deal-breakers (or heartbreakers). Do you feel anxious regularly? Sure, you can take medication (linear thinking) and numb your anxiety each day. But medication won't heal your anxiety disorder. You need to take an in-depth, sometimes painful look at why anxiety hits you so hard or regularly.

Do you feel sorry for homeless people? Sure, you could give them a night in a shelter (linear thinking) and help them have something in their stomach for another day. But tomorrow, they will be hungry again, without a safe and permanent place to call home. Joining a collective effort to promote the creation of permanent housing for these unfortunate folks would bear more long-lasting results.

I'm not saying I don't take medication to alleviate your pain of today or not give shelter to ease today's struggle. I'm only saying that seeking those solutions won't make your life, or the lives of the homeless, better in the long run. Long-term explanations usually take a long time, a lot of effort, and sacrifice. Thus, they are naturally less appealing than the instant gratification that we all look for. We are wired that way as humans. In his book Stumbling on Happiness, Dan Gilbert presented the neuroscientific fact that our ability to think about the future developed somewhere in the past three million years and could be attributed to our frontal lobes fast growth. Before that, our ancestors lived in the "never-ending, present moment." Given the relatively young age of the thinking brain compared to the "reptilian brain," we can conclude our genetic inclination toward wanting something now rather than later is perfectly understandable.

I know that systems problems are complex.

They are not as common as everyday problems.

The problems they cover often seem too big or too overwhelming.

You don't think you have time or knowledge to expand on this thinking method properly.

It often requires more information, teamwork, and higher-level thinking tools.

Do you have other reasons? Please add them to this list. When you are done listing why you shouldn't learn to think in systems, let's examine the list of reasons you should. I'll start with the conclusion of the story of Acme.

Chapter 22:   Strategic Thinking

One of the inherent qualities in any sustainable system is that it must have a clearly defined purpose. Each discrete part must be working in tandem to produce the holistic system and achieve its purpose. Purpose cannot be discerned from the parts themselves; instead, it is derived from how the overarching system works. For example, an oven's purpose is to cook food; this purpose cannot be achieved or detected by merely examining its parts, like the heating coils or the electric supply. Rather, it is the purpose of the oven as a whole, via the interconnectedness of all its parts.

The holistic purpose of a system doesn't mitigate the importance of the attendant parts; indeed, they are crucial to the system's optimal functionality. All of the parts must be present for a system to be achieved. Additionally, all of the parts must be logically ordered and carefully maintained for the system to function smoothly. One missing part or one flaw in the design can prevent a system from working correctly to achieve its planned purpose.

How we perceive how effectively a system is working is through feedback of various kinds. If the food we take out of the oven after a recommended amount of time is not cooked, then we understand that something is wrong with the system. Within an organization, this works in myriad ways: for example, if a product is not selling well or sales begin to drop, then employees rely on feedback from the market, from consumers to discover what in the system has faltered. Thus, the purpose of a system is connected to external factors. The system itself must be functioning properly to achieve its purpose within the parameters of what external forces require or demand.

In mechanical systems made by human design, the purpose is typically clear and explicit. Thus, we know that an oven is made to cook food, so each part is explicitly created to work together with this function in mind. Once all the parts are put together, the system functions as it should for as long as all the parts are working—and the purpose doesn't change. Mechanical systems do not evolve, typically speaking: the oven's next generation may boast better cooking times or extra features, but the purpose is still fundamentally the same. There are some primary exceptions to this in mechanical systems, in that people sometimes use a mechanical system for a function it wasn't designed for. Theoretically, an oven could be used for drying clothes, though because this is not its intended purpose, it could be hazardous—a fire danger, for sure. Understanding the nature of a mechanical system allows us to use it properly and avoid unintended consequences.

Organic systems, on the other hand, are less predictable. Their purpose can change over time, depending on internal and external circumstances. Sometimes those changes are temporary—say, the increase of pollen in an ecosystem during the warmer months—while sometimes the changes are permanent—a butterfly impacts an ecosystem differently than pupae. In any case, living systems are far more complex than mechanical ones, and understanding their purposes can be a perplexing and challenging task. Biological systems don't come with a set of instructions and warnings. Therefore, we often engage with these systems without fully knowing how we affect the system or how our interaction with it might affect us.

For example, certain behaviors that impact our health are not always immediately obvious—the science has to catch up with our knowledge of what certain habits can do to our bodies. Smoking is a prime example of this: for many years, people smoked without knowing the dangers that such behaviors can have on our biological system and the impact to other lives with the release of second-hand smoke. Indeed, smoking was a ritualistic part of religious or social gatherings in many cultures for centuries. But, with the advances made via science, the health dangers of smoking have become abundantly clear. This doesn't mean that everyone heeds these warnings, but it does mean that we know to make an informed decision. It also means that the perception of smoking changes. Once it was an acceptable part of social life or even an important ritual in cultural exchanges, it has become a mostly unacceptable habit to practice in public spaces.

Think also about another fundamental activity in which we all must take part: eating. We eat almost always in no small part determined by what social system we are a part of. It is perfectly acceptable in many parts of the world to eat animals that we might keep as pets in the United States. In other parts of the world, insects make up a large part of people's diets, while those who aren't accustomed to this might find it repulsive.

Problem Solving: Tragedy of the Commons

Self-interest is a fact of human existence—and one that ensures our survival, evolutionarily speaking. However, within complex systems, working for the benefit of the individual or a specialized group can ultimately disrupt the system's successful workings as a whole. As Spock touchingly says at the end of Star Trek: Wrath of Khan, "The film's context is tragic, though the implications for systems' success are not less important. The health and well-being of our social structures and business ventures and our ecosystems are at stake in perpetuating this kind of short-term thinking.

For a less overwhelming example, consider traffic patterns and the infrastructures that either support or impede them. This is both due to the lack of adequate infrastructure and the increasing population density. When everyone decides that he must drive to work and the system is set up wherein most people drive is the same, then it stands to reason that what was once designed as a public good becomes a public nuisance. There are flaws within the system itself, of course—lack of reliable public transportation, no incentives to lessen the appeal of driving (taxation, as in London)—but the other part of the system is also part of the problem, the drivers themselves. Each decision impacts the functionality of the system as a whole.

This happens in dramatic ways in larger systems, as well. Take the example of Venezuela and its current political and economic woes. Because of political corruption and the greed of a powerful few, resources have been mismanaged. One of the most oil-rich states globally, Venezuela should have a booming economy wherein everyone benefits, from the leaders to the everyday citizen. However, under the stewardship of autocrats who thought about their own benefit, the political system was mostly unraveled. Besides, the cascading effect of the political chaos is that the economy is now on the brink of collapse. Inflation has spiraled out of control, both the result of disastrous political policies and individual actions. Typically, in an economy with rapid inflation, sellers start to anticipate more inflation and adjust costs accordingly upward to continue to make a profit. This, in turn, spurs more inflation as other vendors compete to keep up with rising costs. Each actor is working for their benefit, not for the good of the national whole. Just as Venezuela's leaders failed them by investing money in wasteful projects that generated income for themselves and those they favored, individual actors within the communities themselves contribute to a spiraling problem.

The problem with combating the commons' tragedy is that the disagreements about who is to blame or about who is to benefit are rife with conflict. For example, it can be challenging to determine which division within a corporation deserves greater resource allocation. There may be good arguments for disparities within divisions. Still, because all actors in all divisions have a personal interest in keeping or growing their resources, it becomes difficult to compromise. There is scant motivation to give up your slice of the pie. It is only when there is an agreement that each division should coordinate to work for the collective whole that there can be progress made, and systems mapping is one way to do it.

First, there are a series of compelling questions to ask of all stakeholders to determine what the collective goals are and how best to reach them. What, if any, incentives are available to offer individuals who persist in standing their ground? That is, there must be a way to show employees that their vested interest should be in the company as a whole rather than in their own division's success or their compensation. Who controls those incentives? And are they being responsive to reasonable requests? Is there a significant time delay before individuals can reap the benefits of their efforts? This could be a clear indication that the problem is one of communication and transparency. Is it possible to show that the loss to the collective whole is more impactful than the loss to the individual division or stakeholder? Are there limits to the resources currently being allocated? If so, is there a way that workers can be incentivized to change this in a positive direction? That is, how can resources be replenished in a way that would make everyone more invested in the collective?

As in all systems thinking, the answers are context-specific and require every part's goodwill and effort within the larger whole. The leverage that can be attained is reconciling the short-term individual goals with the long-term collective good: a systems map is an excellent way to create a visual image of how resource allocation feeds into a holistic goal. Reevaluating incentives and fostering coordination are ways in which to combat this systemic problem.

Chapter 23:   Forming Good Habits that Last

You want to be successful. It's the whole reason you've read this book to this point. I applaud you for that. I assume that you now understand the importance of thinking about the long term in your quest for success. You get that you've got to be disciplined for you to conquer milestone after milestone along your journey. The only method to move up the ladder of success is by constantly repeating the things that work, one rung at a time. In other words, to succeed, it all comes down to your habits.

If you want to start up a new business or improve your health, you must make sure you have the right habits. The question is, how can you not just replace bad habits with good ones, but also make them permanent? First, we're going to take a critical look at all the things people get wrong about habits.

Myths about Building Habits

"It takes 21 days for you to form a habit." How many times have you heard that one? Well, that's not the way it goes. There's no proper research backing that up. Before you argue, reread the last sentence and notice the word 'proper' is in bold letters.

Real research on how time-consuming it takes to form a habit suggests that many variables could affect how long it takes you to form a habit, from your environment to the habit, to your kind of person, among other things. I guess there's no way to spin that into a great book title, so many people preach that 21 days' hogwash.

You shouldn't be thinking of habits in light of how long it takes you to form them, anyway. If you do that, you'll notice that you're missing out on the point behind creating better habits to begin with: Creating lasting change in your life. It's a lifestyle thing, not a 21-day fad. You're not going to get results by crossing off each new day on your calendar. Now that I've sufficiently dashed your dreams of becoming a better person in three weeks, the question becomes, how exactly can you make sure your new habits stick?

Micro Targets and Macro Goals

Let's talk about motivation for a minute. Research has found that if you want to be more disciplined, you would be better off with abstract thinking. In other words, you can dream big. You can be all about the big picture and forget about the minutiae.

With that said, many people are uncomfortable with making plans they deem too grand, and as such, they get scared of the size of their dreams and their expectations, thinking there's more of a chance to fail than succeed. Sound familiar?

Lots of research shows that when you are motivated to make something happen by intrinsic elements, versus extrinsic elements like the anticipation of a reward or the fear of punishment, you will be able to stick with your goals and habits. You will find ways to walk the fine line between being a big dreamer and doing the little things every day that get you closer to that big dream of yours. That means when you're intrinsically motivated to make your goals happen, you're cool with not having dramatic, overnight changes. It's just going to come over a while.

With all of that said, to create habits that stick, you need to have micro targets and macro goals. While the goals are the big picture, the targets are the little things you must do each day to make your goal happen.

Targets make it easy for you to stay on course each day. They help you achieve your goal. Here's the best thing about achieving your goal with targets: The best kinds of targets are the shallow ones. You could commit to writing just 100 words a day if you're an aspiring author. You could write

101, or even go so far as to write 5000 in a day if you're feeling a bit fired up, but the point is you just need to write 100. As you do this, you're teaching yourself a new habit. Sure, you may only ever write 100 words a day now and then, but for the most part, chances are you're hitting 5 or 10 times that target.

On Plans, Triggers, and Changes in Behavior

Habits and planning go hand in hand. See, most people talk about a new habit they want to adopt, but rarely do you ever hear them mention why they want to make that new habit a thing.

I know it doesn't seem like much; however, this helps you remain motivated every day. You're less likely to stick with it if all you do is think about it. Also, don't just start in on a new habit without being clear about what you want to achieve. If you do, you will begin to lose your resolve, and you won't be consistent.

Recent research shows that while visualizing positively helps keep you motivated and inspired, it's not enough. It's a matter of what you visualize. You visualize yourself working out, taking stairs instead of the elevator, saying no to junk food, eating healthy, and so on. This is the way to give your new habit the stickiness you need to achieve your goal.

For another, when you visualize each of the steps you need to take, you find that you're less anxious about it and are more likely to consider it a possible thing for you to stick with your new habit as part of your lifestyle.

Habits You Should Practice Daily to Stay Productive

You need to get habits in place so that when you run out of motivation, they will kick in automatically, and you'll still be on the right track. When you have the habits in place, it's easy to find motivation even if you're not feeling it… And you won't have to force it. Here are some habits to form that can keep you motivated and productive.

Visualize. You have no idea just how powerful visualization is. Take time to visualize your goals and your future at the start of your day, and you will find yourself feeling inspired to push through with your target. All you need is three minutes a day, using the 3-phase visualization technique. In phase 1, consider what you'd like to be like for you within the next 3 to 5 years. See what you've done, what you're doing, who you're with, and where you are. In phase 2, see the next 12 months and what they have in store for you. In phase 3, see what you have to get started on today so that you can make your dreams come true.

Go over your goals. Do this each day, and last thing before bed. Go over why you're doing what you do and what you need to do to achieve them. Not only will you feel motivated, but you will also be able to stay focused and have brilliant ideas on how you can get there.

Take cold showers. If you're having trouble becoming fully awake, or if you're having trouble focusing, then take a cold shower. Once you do, you feel motivated and ready to perform. Make a habit of cold morning showers. It's not pleasant at first, but when you step out, you're more than ready to take charge of your day. Just remain calm, do some deep breathing, and detach your mind from how your skin feels. Give it 15 to 20 seconds, and it will become obvious the cold is not as bad as you dreaded.

Read. Read something. Every day. I find I feel off if I don't get some reading in. When you read, your brain will have a lot of material to work with and give you fresh new ideas to inspire you to greatness. Make it a habit to read in the morning and the evening.

Use affirmations. These are messaging you repeat to yourself every day so that you remember what you're trying to achieve. You can leave yourself notes where you'll see them, keep your affirmations in your wallet, or as a reminder on your phone. Affirmations are messaged you find motivating and empowering. They can be famous quotes or your mantra.

Make your environment work for you. This will require some adaptability and flexibility on your part, especially when you're in a challenging environment. Your environment will always influence your productivity levels.

Develop the habit of NOW. Got an idea? Go test it out now. Notice there's something you just have to do? Why not now? There's only ever now. You can tell yourself you'll do it later, but the truth is when later rolls around, it will still be now anyway! So why not does it this now so you can use the next now to do something else? That's how to remain productive.

Chapter 24:   Intellectual Development

The most basic education levels feature a state whereby the students are said to be in Dualism or a state of Received knowledge. In this primary stage, the learner's understanding is based on either acknowledging fact or disapproving fiction. Here, knowledge of a concept depends on one's skill to remember the subject's events. The teacher's part is to deliver facts while the learner must learn and relay the facts during an examination.

Their learner is bound to get frustrated as this stage involves getting to know a concept without a factual basis. This leads to the next level, which is referred to as subjective knowledge. This stage entails the memorizing of all the dimensions relative to a particular subject. However, this is an uphill approach that eventually facilitates understanding that learners possess valuable ideologies even when they are seen to have disparities in argument within themselves, with the tutors, and with the books.

This stage's dangerous threat is that learners are confused by disparity view-point and conception of situations, a condition described as intellectual paralysis. However, for the ideologies to be applicable in the real world, the learner needs to adopt a particular part of thinking and a different manner of viewing various aspects of life. This equips the learner with the ability to pick a specific line of thought. This may be a temporary influence, which is subject to change according to the situation but is more advantageous to the learner than the initial stages of the uncertainty of perception. This is a highly advanced level of understanding and comprehension and is usually only achieved by a few of the accomplished scholars who can make that level in limited exposure to advanced education levels.

Social Identity Development

This is defined as the mental process through which we perceive or acknowledge our social identities or our status in society. Every person desires to identify their place in the community. These social groupings are classified as either stigmatized or a dominant cluster. They serve as platforms for an individual to discover one's social identity and to cultivate a sense of belonging in society. Researchers in this field have observed the relationship between these processes of perception and the learning process.

According to research, these two pathways share similar characteristics. In this case, children are observed to exhibit naivety in perspective in the earlier stages of development, for instance, being able to distinguish skin color or other physical attributes but not characterize these attributes to the person's character or personality. Soon, they become bombarded with external views and experiences that open their minds to the character traits of the most appropriate figures, the best lifestyle trends, and the best insights in life. These insights are universal, and as such, are many times accepted as exhibiting both stigmatized and dominant characteristics.

These learners challenge these external influences and views when injustices are committed or through interactions with other groups in meaningful ways. For most people, college is still the first significant interaction with people of diverse social positions, grouped collaborations whereby information and content about specific fields become the motivator for the questioning process. This process differs according to the stages. The stigmatized members in society find themselves in the immersion stage. They try to find comparative avenues to share their experiences with friends and peers, enabling them to curb social anomalies like racism, among other delinquencies in society.

On the other hand, members of dominant groups enter the Disintegration stage. Here, they face the oppressive history of their group. Their perception of their identity in society is challenged and disintegrates, forcing them to restructure their manners of understanding and comprehension of their character. Both processes can bear the pain and extreme guilt and anger feelings. The individuals who develop continuously can create a positive sense of self during the Internalization and Redefinition stages. They discover that social realization is only a single aspect of one's entire self.

Many learners at the college level are stuck at the acceptance, immersion, and disintegration phases, which breed more confusion during course evaluation. This conflict will affect the entire course climate and retard the learning process unless it is absorbed and directed into a beneficial talk about

Course Climate

Learners utilize the course contexts as they work out their developmental activities. It is, therefore, crucial to creating a learning environment that conducive to the learning process. A study based on the female gender was initially used to draw attention to the learning climate through the "chilly climate" articles, which back in the '80s featured the learning climate for female students appertaining to higher educational levels. However, research studies have provided conclusive evidence of an unfriendly environment's adverse effects on students' learning, career orientation, and critical thinking. Desire and Church have explained how a learner's perception is affected directly or indirectly by the learning climate.

Strategies

Educators cannot force development but instead can only encourage it. If this development can be promoted, it can improve the course climate and make learning more conducive. Universal principles can be formulated, and disciplinary approaches will remain useful.

To push students from Dualism, it is essential first to inspire uncertainty in their thinking. The learners need to bear the possibility to nurture flexibility and adaptability in their perceptions and approaches to problems.

Evidence is useful in promoting the learner from standard multiplicity. To change their perspective from relativism, it is vital to study the consequences and relative values that are integrated with each process to give them full responsibility for their thinking processes.

The teachers should compare their perceptions regarding the course progress against the students' perspective since the course climate is all about proper understanding. Responses to questions may differ, but these disparities can be sorted out. The correlations between students and teachers are a significant determinant of the learning climate, mostly affecting the learners who are on the verge of quitting their study lines. The teachers whom students feel as being more open, approachable, helpful, and friendly create better and more inspiring earning climates.

A conducive learning climate can also be influenced by the relationships between students and fellow students. This is mostly applicable in extensive courses whereby student-student interaction is limited. The tutors are required to promote these student interactions through group associations and collaborative learning management systems to create better learning climates.

The tone of information delivery also affects the climate. Different hues of expressing a similar point produce differences in the learner's perceptions of the course due to the tutor's approachability and appeal to help the student in learning. This determines the student's willingness, especially in seeking further guidance from the tutor regarding the subject in question. This aspect mostly affects newer learners at various levels of education.

We need to know how to study and be flexible in our learning approaches to be self-directed students.

The key to a self-directed approach is through practicing meta-cognition. This promotes independent and goal-oriented thinking and enables self-reflection of one's learning activities. Achieving this understanding requires developing "executive functioning" strategies, which allows one to be in charge of own thinking processes. Meta-cognition entails planning, monitoring, and evaluation of the student's learning and perceptive abilities. The learner in this stage can practice self-reflection and is aware of the limits of the known and unknown factors in their study. The students are also equipped with plenty of learning abilities that they can apply in the process, including determining how and when to use the concepts and the adaptability to change of strategy if either approach fails. They can analyze their results, highlight mistakes and errors in their work, and practice the newly learned procedures to tackle the next challenges.

According to the findings of Ambrose, Bridges, Dippier, Lovett, and Norman, the responsibility that the student has to be a self-directed learner is to learn how to make accurate assessments of the requirements of each task and evaluations of their acquired skills and knowledge. They also need to strategize their approaches and adjust to strategy in different situations while monitoring their progress. Research has long identified such behavior as a possible academic success indicator at all academic levels. With the increased learning demands at the college level, it is essential to have learning approaches that transcend passive knowledge and memorization. In most cases, students are seen as unprepared to apply the meta-cognitive strategies applied in college levels of education. This factor applies even to accomplished students, especially those who grew without enough challenging situations, which are vital for developing meta-cognitive abilities.

Research shows that these skills are acquired best in the context of the courses. Once learning methods are combined with the content, the learner can efficiently translate them to tasks and monitor that translation outcome. By integrating different metacognitive strategies in the course work, instructors greatly assist students in developing their thinking processes.

Planning for Learning

For learning to be effective, the initial focus should be on planning. Accomplished students spend a great deal of time and resources during the planning process, an effort whose importance is hardly realized by the

novice learners. Students should learn the importance of prior planning

during the learning process.

Chapter 25:   Smart Decision Thinking

Problem-solving is that term that has found its place in most fields. For example, in psychology, problem-solving would be defined as finding a solution to any mental issues or processes. In contrast, statistics would be described as a method to answer a specific question on how many fish are there in a lake.

One must remember that the problems can also be categorized. These categories would be well-defined and ill-defined problems.

Ill-defined problems, as the name suggests, are problems that do not have a clear-cut goal. It makes it challenging to come up with solutions to such issues. You might not be able to identify an expected answer. These problems have well-defined goals, making it easier to estimate the problem's magnitude and identify feasible solutions to the same. We might also be able to plan if we recognize such a problem.

When you are faced with a problem in any field, or even in your life, you might either solve the problem through logic or try to interpret the question. No matter which method you use, you have to first understand the problem's goal and try to identify the different routes you can take to solve the problem. This is the key to problem-solving! You might sometimes have to resort to abstract thinking and try coming up with a creative solution.

For instance, consider that you teach a bunch of 10-year-old English. You have to cover the different parts of speech in an hour. You know that the children that you teach have a low attention span. Your problem here is to grab the kids' attention for an hour to help them understand the parts of speech. You could either go about regularly teaching them using the text or make fun of them! This is a problem where you would use abstract thinking to find a creative solution. You know that your children love games. So, you can come up with a brilliant game that they will enjoy. But ensure that this game also teaches them the parts of speech!

Critical thinking is a knowledgeable skill, and it can benefit those who become adept at using it in every decision they make. As a critical thinker, one of your goals is to become more familiar with your subconscious mind and learn about the knowledge base mechanics that resides there.

Critical thinkers know that arguments are created in such a way for people to have means of determining the validity of everything that happens in the world. In most situations, you may not even know whether you could make the whole argument in proving that a claim is valid or not. However, the way you argue would be the one that would count.

Problem Solver Qualities

Be Open-Minded

Do not go into a situation to be the 'hero' or 'savior.' This will only serve to cloud your judgment because you will take it upon yourself to provide all the solutions. A critical thinker knows that his or his approach is not the only one, and it may not be the best; hence, it is the importance of being open-minded. When you are open-minded, you will listen to others and seek solutions that will work best, even when the answers are not something you provided.

Empathetic

To improve your problem-solving skills, you must look outside yourself. Empathy allows you to do this; it removes internal focus from your biases and shifts it towards someone else. When this happens, you begin to see situations through the eyes of someone else as it were. If you are empathetic, you will also improve your communication skills, your people skills (cooperation with other people), and your ability to work with others.

Problem-solving should not use emotions, faulty, or incomplete information as to its basis. Instead, it should use rational considerations as its base. This means that you need to find out what is truly going on and gather all information before making any judgments. Your solutions should use facts and evidence as to their base. Your own opinion and emotions should not hinder your taste.

Problem-solving simply entails finding solutions to different situations, problems, and challenges you face. It is an extremely crucial skill to build and improve because practical problem solving helps you combat challenges, ease your struggles, and find innovative fixes to the most bizarre and seemingly unfixable problems.

Besides, problem-solving is a lifesaver when it comes to making decisions. If your problem-solving skills are excellent, you will likely make a well-thought-out and foolproof decision quickly and easily.

Nobody has excellent problem-solving skills at birth; we learn these skills and build them over time.

Personal Decision-Making Styles

Directive Style

If your decision-making style is directive, it means you value structure above all else. You are aggressive and expect instant results whenever you give an order. When you encounter a problematic situation, you take charge, make fast decisions,

As a directive decision-maker, you have learned to depend entirely on your experience, knowledge, judgment, and information. You are a perfectionist for the rules and have excellent verbal skills to give clear directions.

However, there are some limitations to this style of making decisions. You tend to act very quickly without waiting for all the facts. This means that you are likely to make rash decisions without assessing other alternatives. It is also possible that your choices provide short-term benefits but no long-term solutions.

Analytic Style

If this is your style of making decisions, then you are a born problem-solver. You just love examining all kinds of problems, challenges, and puzzles and figuring them out. You are innovative and enjoy dealing with large quantities of data whenever required to make a decision. Analysis-paralysis means nothing to you. No matter how challenging the problem is, you are adaptable enough to handle it all.

On the flip side, however, you are also a slow decision-maker. You tend to wait for all the data and events to come in before making a move means your decision-making process can be very time-consuming. To some extent, some people may describe you as a control freak.

Conceptual Style

As a conceptual decision-maker, you see problems from an artistic perspective. You tend to be very creative when solving problems. You try as much as possible to come up with solutions that are fresh and new. Unlike a directive decision-maker, you believe that every solution must be long-term. You try to think about how your current decisions will impact the future. As a result, you are a risk-taker and extremely achievement-oriented.

Behavioral Style

You are a natural peacemaker who believes that every decision must bring people together and avoid conflict. You are very diplomatic and excel at persuading people to see your point of view. Since you are a people-person, you prefer to work in a group to agree on the best action to take. This allows you to help people reconcile their differences and agree on one acceptable solution.

Group Decision-Making Styles

Autocratic Style

This is a decision-making style where you, as the leader of a group, take total control of every decision. You don't even bother to ask your group members for their opinion or ideas on how to solve the problem. You simply decide what to do, depending on your perception and internal information. As a result, you are held entirely responsible for your decision's positive and negative outcomes.

The autocratic style of decision-making is instrumental when the group needs to make a quick decision, for example, during an emergency. However, this style also brings many challenges within the group.

Group members may not be enthusiastic about implementing a decision that was made without their input. For example, if the decision affects employees negatively, morale will go down, and they will become resentful toward the manager. Therefore, the company's productivity will be affected, and the manager may no longer be seen as a credible leader.

Democratic Style

This particular style allows you to make quick decisions by involving the entire group. As the leader, you give up your control and ownership of decision-making and enable group members to vote. The resolution that gets the majority of the vote will be adopted and implemented by everyone.

The problem with this style is that, unlike the autocratic style, there is no sense of individual responsibility. No single member can be held responsible for any decision the group makes. If something goes wrong, one member may refuse to accept responsibility because they voted against the resolution in the first place.

Collective Style

This is where the leader of a group gets everyone's input about the situation and involves the members in every step of the process. However, the final decision rests with you alone. You encourage your group members to share their ideas and any information they may have about the situation. As they do this, you gain greater insight and a wide range of perspectives on how the problem may be solved. You analyze the input you have received and make your decision.

In the characteristic style of group decision-making, you have to accept full responsibility for the outcome of your decision. The benefit of this style is that everyone gets the chance to participate in the process. To succeed as a leader, you must develop excellent communication skills and become a good listener. This is the best technique for you to get a clear picture of the situation and make the best decision possible. On the other hand, the fact that you have to wait for group input makes the decision-making process very slow.

Consensus Style

This is quite similar to the democratic style, but what makes them different is that the decision must be unanimous in the consensus style of decision-making. As a leader, you have no control over the final decision and do not have to accept individual responsibility for the outcome. Everyone must agree. Otherwise, the decision cannot be regarded as consensual.

The most important value of this style is that it creates a strong sense of commitment within the group. Everyone feels like their opinion matters and plays a part in the success of the group. By involving every single member of the group, you will increase the likelihood of achieving success. The consensual decision-making style is usually used when you have a small group of people working together for an extended period. An excellent example of this is a business partnership.

The only downside is that the decision-making process will be slow. It is also challenging to teach a group of people to work together like this and still maintain harmony.

Chapter 26:   Places to Intervene in A System

There are numerous places for systems thinkers that help out in almost any scenario. While many of them have been discussed in abstract ways throughout the book, this Segment will focus on the specific categories of places and some methods to use them effectively. While all of these places can easily stand alone, they also work very effectively in cooperation with one another in the spirit of systems thinking.

There are four broad categories of systems thinking places, from the familiar to the innovative. Brainstorming places are ones that most of us have used at one time or another during our academic years or professional lives. Dynamic thinking places are also familiar to us, even if the name is not; these are the looping diagrams that show relationships and interactions between elements. Occasionally, these are reminiscent of a coach's description of a team's strategic plays. Essential thinking places are graphs and diagrams that lay the foundation for more complex models, such as our last category. Computer-based places are technological aides that run the gamut from learning laboratories to flight simulators; Simultaneously, these require high proficiency levels to create, they are efficiently utilized by anyone who has adequate training.

Brainstorming places are used in the early stages of creating a system or diagnosing a problem within an existing system. One of the simple of these is something that almost every English teacher at one point in time encourages his students to do: the cluster diagram. This layout places the central topic in the middle of a page and then has the individual or group associate ideas around the clusters' central one. This is the organization's initial stage, wherein you are identifying the common elements within a particular system. From there, you can begin to see patterns and interrelationships.

Another brainstorming tool that can help see interactions and overlaps among parts is the old-school Boolean tool (this is the logic on which most search engines operate). Usually depicted as two interlocking circles, wherein there is one idea to the left, one idea to the right, and a middle piece where the two meet and overlap. This kind of model allows you to explore the relationship between two concepts: is it an "and" relationship? An "or" relationship? A "not" relationship? Searching for African "and" American will yield quite different results than searching for African "not" Americans, to use quite a general example. This tool helps you define the parameters of the system you intend to utilize. It can also be extended into interlocking circle designs, wherein you see the complexities of the interactions among many different terms and parts.

Dynamic thinking places go beyond simple linear graphs to show how events and information work in multi-directional ways. For example, a "behavior over time" graph charts different variables to explain how A, B, C, and so on interact with one another over some time. A causal loop diagram can be used in conjunction with the "behavior over time" graph to chart how reinforcing and balancing loops work within the system. A systems archetype diagram is the visual equivalent of explaining the dynamic interactions within complex systems: many of these have been explored within the book, such as drifting goals fixes that fail and shifting the burden. These archetypes are most useful in identifying the fundamental source of a problem rather than responding to the immediate symptom.

Essential thinking places include graphical function diagrams, which show how one variable affects another, plotting the full range of relevant interactions over time and within context. The policy structure diagram, which essentially maps the decision-making processes within an organization, can structure an entire organization and allocate resources within it. Another example of an essential thinking tool is the structure-behavior pair, which provides the building blocks for the computer-based places. These can include exponential growth, S-shaped growth, and other models that are genuinely three dimensional.

Computer-based places allow us to map out what we would like our system to look like and make predictions based on variable factors and play them out in virtual time. These allow you to run policy analyses of long-term projects and project growth and resource needs. There are also the flight simulator models geared toward training management to deal with the company's every day running and the potential crisis that crops up. Last, learning laboratories combine most of the systems thinking places within a computer simulation to train interactively.

Collaborative ways of thinking and working take time and creating a system that encapsulates the methodologies of systems thinking is a process, not an event. There are two fundamental ways to respond to an ever-changing world: when events happen, you can react, or, with knowledge of how functions work, you can be a participating actor instead of a passive reactor. When a machine breaks down, we respond by trying to fix it. With systems thinking, you begin to develop an ability to predict when and why the machine will break down, therefore giving yourself an edge in strategic planning and decision making. With these places at your disposal, your ability to transform your organization or your worldview is enabled.

Chapter 27:   Understand Bottlenecks, Leverage, and Feedback Loops

If everything is interconnected, it stands to reason that there is (or should be) a flow of information between and among the parts of the holistic system. Communication should occur not only from a position of authority to a place of subordinate but in reverse as well. Communication should occur not only among bosses and employees but between employees themselves. If an organization fails to acknowledge feedback or create open communication channels, then the system on which it depends will inevitably break down.

Within systems thinking, there are two main types of feedback loops that are frequently talk about reinforcing and balancing. While we usually have positive associations with the concept of "reinforcement," in terms of systems thinking, reinforcing feedback loops are primarily negative: virtually, a reinforcing loop function to maintain more of the same, rather than re-think the system re-engage with problems to create novel solutions. For example, when water flows over a dam or a riverbank, it erodes the very structure, human-made or natural, that is supposed to keep it contained, creating more of the same—that is, flooding. When reinforcing loops occur within an organizational system, it can lead to stagnation and waste. Resources are invested in the same tired ideas that haven't provided solutions in the first place. Exceptions to the negative associations with reinforcing loops are when feedback serves to foster trust and loyalty to an organization; as people gain confidence and lose fear; they become more productive participants in the organization as a whole.

The second type of feedback loop is a balancing loop. This is when the parts within the system work together to maintain a productive and successful balance. An example of this is how nature has solved the predator versus prey situation: larger predator animals weed out smaller prey, thus controlling the population while breeding in lower numbers. Suppose this system gets out of balance via uncontrolled hunting, habitat destruction, environmental events, and one kind of animal reproduction unchecked. In that case, the system gets out of balance, leading to many adverse outcomes. A balancing feedback loop encourages stability and sustainability within the method wherein (as in the Forgoing example) everyone has equal access to territory and food. In terms of a human-constructed system, such as markets, a balancing feedback loop ensures that supply and demand will be relatively stable; for many who use methods thinking to work toward social justice, a balancing feedback loop will allow for communication between the privileged, dominant class and the disenfranchised and marginalized. This includes fostering relationships between philanthropic organizations, governmental agencies, and local actors. Often, a healthy system working with a balancing feedback loop will be self-correcting.

Causality

The talk concerning feedback loops in the Forgoing piece is really about understanding causality. There are issues of cause and effect; the better able we are to identify how one part of the system affects another, the better we are to anticipate potential problems and make decisions to prevent them. Cause and effect are simple concepts taught from a very young age: actions have consequences, or activities have results. The key in a complex system is in determining how the parts impact each other within the system.

Since change is a constant, part of the challenge in deciphering causality is keeping up with the flux and flow of the system. One particular way to understand causality from systems thinking perspective is to create a causal loop diagram wherein you can identify how each piece affects each other and the system. In this loop, there are variables, the links between the variables, the explanations of how the variables are linked, and the result of those interactive parts—how the system will ultimately behave. A more straightforward way of thinking about it is to state the obvious: causality is a way of understanding how things, people, activities, and events link together to create an outcome.

Another essential feature of causality is that, contrary to the basic examples one might have learned back in secondary school, no one causes leads to one effect, typically speaking. There are multiple causes in any complex system, and the results that come from these causes can be determined by making different choices based on each variable. For example, in mechanistic, linear thinking, you might see a vehicular accident such as a car crash (cause) results in the insurance claim (effect). However, in systems thinking, such linearity negates the complexity of cause and potential response. What caused the crash? A tire blows out (root), so the driver loses control of the car (object); therefore, crashing into another vehicle (cause). Thus, an insurance claim is filed (effect). The multiple reasons are critical to the impact because the insurance claim will be determined based on the cause of the crash. You can even look further back: was the tire defective? Who installed it? It can also be examined psychologically: car crash (cause) results in anxiety over driving (force) and leads to overly cautious driving, making you late for work (effect). Each

link in the chain is part of the rippling effect of causality. Ultimately, it is

not a simple linear chart but rather an interactive story that recognizes how

the multiple parts of any system create particular outcomes.

Chapter 28:   Creating Change-In Systems

To understand how best to plan for the future, it is imperative to understand how systems behave. Among the most superficially different operation types, there are underlying systemic behaviors that we can discern common to most. Indeed, feedback loops are a crucial part of that commonality. There are lessons to be learned about how to decode a system by witnessing other networks' failures and how feedback loops contribute to that process. On its surface, feedback is a simple concept: listen to the stakeholders within the system to see what might be changed to better the system. However, understanding feedback within complex systems requires a little more exploration.

To use some generalized examples, we have all witnessed the collapse of an initially hugely successful business that seems to implode overnight. Or, we have seen (or participated in) the endless cycle of weight loss and weight gain, the same fifteen or twenty pounds gained and lost in a frustrating loop. Or, we have struggled to host a Thanksgiving dinner devoid of negative family interactions. At least one of these scenarios will ring a familiar bell for most of us.

These very different examples all contain certain commonalities, particularly the various feedback loops that either set us up to succeed or lead to failure. The two feedback loops crucial to understanding systems are reinforcing loops and balancing loops. Indeed, these are the very building blocks of dynamic systems structures.

In the case of reinforcing loops, we find that these contribute to both positive growths, and in many cases, eventual collapse. This feedback loop begins positively by recognizing success within the system—the business is growing; profits are increasing—which encourages the system's parts to maintain the status quo. Management, workers, the means of production are all reinforced to stay the same. Concomitantly, this means that growth and change are happening only in one direction. This is like having a savings account: each month, the interest accrues you have positive growth in additional savings (this assumes you aren't withdrawing, of course). However, this reinforcing loop can lead to sedentary behavior. It's great that the savings account grows incrementally with monthly interest. Still, it doesn't necessarily encourage you to invest more money into the said account or diversify said account to accrue more interest. Nevertheless, this positive growth is at least a movement in the right direction.

When reinforcing loops grow truly stagnant, though, as, within an organization, it fails to notice changes that require new and different responses, for example, if a company creates a product that is suddenly in high demand, then the company must respond to this not by reinforcing the same behaviors that led to that demand. In fact, without changes to the means of production and distribution, this can lead to underproduction and, eventually, a reputation for not reliably meeting demand. (Paradoxically, scarcity can sometimes increase demand.) It can also lead to complacency wherein the original best-selling item is redesigned by a competitor who has been more carefully watching the market, thus rendering your product obsolete. Just because your innovative system produced success doesn't mean that it will continue to do so without further developing ideas and investment of resources.

With balancing loops, the system is encouraged to reach a state of stability, wherein demand does not outstrip supply, nor does the amount overwhelm demand. These balancing loops take us out of reinforcing loops' linear thinking, where the outcomes are increased growth or slow decline. Balancing loops work multi-directionally and encourage communication at and between every level.

When a system is in balance, it has the original goal of achieving a specific performance level. Tesla is an example of a company that has appeared to be recently out of balance, promising mid-priced cars by a particular date without having the strategic planning in place to deliver—too few workers and assembly lines that were overworked for too long. Tesla grew too fast to make good on its promises.

A system in balance is one in which a strategic plan is explicitly articulated in the service of a particular vision. Indeed, what fuels the balancing loop is the gap between the ideal goals and the actual performance; thus, you need clear goals and clear strategies even to begin to recognize the differences. The system is built to be self-reinforcing, like a thermostat in your house: when the air is cold enough or warm enough, the system shuts itself off until the desired temperature starts to drop or rise restarts itself, maintaining a reasonably constant temperature. This is how an ideally balanced system works.

Balancing systems are common in nature and human-designed systems, but we don't always notice them because they are quietly keeping things in a happy balance. When we begin to see problems, we recognize that something in the system is flawed enough to interrupt the balancing loops.

This is when we speak of "damage control": something has disrupted the normal flow of events. We must step in to analyze the system to determine which parts are no longer contributing to the system's overall function.

The other important element within the idea of balancing feedback loops is that it encourages better and more egalitarian communication. Instead of managers and board members calling all the shots about how the system is set up, the workers and producers are also called upon to give their perspectives. Diversifying the feedback will assist in identifying the gaps within the system before they lead to irreversible damage. For example, a worker on the production line might suggest that they slow down production; from his perspective, the work is too fast-paced, or the output is too large for the shrinking demand. She might suggest that they invest more resources into hiring more production line workers or improving the line's efficiency for a manager. The worker knows the conditions on the ground, as it were, while the manager is more aware of the resources that can be allotted to fix the gaps that are throwing the system out of balance. By working together, a long-term solution can finally be addressed.

Chapter 29:   Drifting Goals

One of our most human tendencies is that of procrastination. We set goals with every admirable intention to meet them, to meet them in a timely fashion, to make more goals promptly following that. But, as with anything worthwhile, these goals can be challenging and complex, complicated by external factors that we cannot control and internal factors that require re-adjustment from time to time. Within systems thinking, "drifting goals" is one archetypes that helps us defend against an ever down-sliding scale from the best of intentions to the most mediocre of outcomes.

The analogy of the "boiling frog" is often used when talking about drifting goals. It goes something like this: a frog is dropped into a pot of boiling water, and instinct being what it is, immediately leaps out of the container; thus, the frog is saved, but dinner is ruined (assuming that you eat frogs for dinner; if not, substitute lobster). The frog has fallen victim to a kind of numb state that represents the case of drifting goals. This structure allows for incremental changes in performance (temperature, in the analogy) that eventually result in disaster (for the frog). If our goal is survival—financially, personally, socially—then we must beware of the tendency toward drifting goals. From an organizational standpoint, the changes occur so incrementally that we might not notice them until it's too late: delivery is a week late, but it starts to happen with regularity, so it becomes acceptable; the week becomes two, then three, and so on; the pace loses its urgency—until it's down to panic mode and the lack of precision and quality that accompany such a state.

Of course, adjusting goals is not inherently wrong—the "slippery slope" argument is indeed a logical fallacy. A shift in your goals, personally or professionally, does not always spell disaster; in fact, it may indicate even greater future success. The difficulty is determining when a shift in goals is a necessary response to external factors and internal pressures or a slow slide into mediocrity and, ultimately, failure.

One of the ways to envision this difference is to picture the drifting goal in two different loops: in one circuit, the goal is immediately lowered, therefore closing the gap between the original purpose and the actual reality; in another course, the unmet goal is addressed through corrective action, which doesn't immediately close the gap between ideal and practical, but can be a more lasting solution. Take deadlines as a particularly apt example: the goal is set for the production of X number of units in X amount of time, but for whatever reason, it becomes clear that X amount of time is not enough. The quickest fix is to extend the deadline, therefore lowering the goal itself. This happens in large organizations that tend to lose sight of the overall system; the lack of performance and the excess of unmet goals aren't noticed until it's too late.

Taking corrective action—before it's too late—is fundamental to avoiding the problems created by drifting goals. The frog becomes too accustomed to the warming water—he is not paying attention to what is happening around him—until he is lured into a disastrous state of apathy. This is why setting goals, devising a strategic plan, creating feedback loops, and following up on all of the above is necessary. In systems thinking, the focus is not merely on the result (X amount of merchandise produced) and on the process and quality of the said result.

One of the keys to addressing drifting goals before they lead to disastrous results is understanding where the pressure is coming to modify the goals: is it external pressure (falling customer demand)? Or internal expectations (performance based on past versus performance based on objective standards)? This requires a fundamental understanding of how the system works. Customer demand is external to the system, but the policy can be an evaluation to respond to those external pressures: if fewer customers are requesting the product, evaluation of the quality, competition, and marketing would be in order. Internal expectations are more within the purview of organizational control. If deadlines are drifting because they are being charted by past performance, then perhaps an assessment of expectations is in order. If deadlines are drifting because of an absolute standard that hasn't been adequately explained or realistically considered, then a revamping of those deadlines is necessary. This is mostly about working backward from a goal: why was the original goal left unmet, and what can you do about it?

From a personal viewpoint, it can be easy to locate the problem of drifting goals, though not always objectively easy to solve them, as so many things can come into play. Suppose you're trying to learn a new skill, for example. In that case, your original goal can be confounded by external events—job and family responsibilities—and internal factors—an overreach out of optimism or an unforeseen personal roadblock. In either of these cases, it may be perfectly acceptable to regroup and reframe your goals. It may also be a matter of its principle to regroup and recommit to those goals. The most crucial issue to keep in mind is that drifting goals inevitably leads to loss of productivity and potential failure. The question when dealing with them is to ask yourself what's at stake? My desire to memorize Homer's the Odyssey may ultimately be an unrealistic and unimportant goal in the grand scheme of things. Meeting merchandise quote at the company I founded may be a crucial and life-affecting goal. Fixing the problem requires the time and effort to take corrective actions and see them through.

Chapter 30: Solving Every Day and Complex Problems

One of the most significant impediments to emergence is faulty problem-solving. When we stay mired in traditional, linear ways of thinking, we become stuck in the cycle of reacting to events and problems rather than pro-actively examining the system to determine the cause of the problem. Fixing an individual problem within a system is usually only momentarily addressing a symptom of a more significant systemic issue. Think about the squeaky wheel analogy: it gets the grease, yes, but what if it needs a new axle to help it turn smoothly? The symptom (squeakiness) will eventually rise again because the surface fix does not address the system's needs.

We are often caught in the cycle of fighting fires rather than clearing the forest floor (or, in more modern solutions, allowing the ecological system to make itself of debris by managing fires, a solution that addresses the system rather than the symptom). Frequently, in our haste to solve a surface problem, we find that it worsens the matter in the long term.

Think of this in terms of personal health. When you have a cold, the systemic issue is not the coughing and the stuffy nose—these are the symptoms—but rather the invading virus that revs up our immune system, causing our body to expel the bad stuff. While the common cold is not a significant health event, it is worth noting that misdiagnoses occur when doctors don't know what extent of the system in a holistic way. If someone presents with hypertension, say, how does the doctor know the most effective treatment method without knowing the whole story? Hypertension can be hereditary (biological system), initiated by stress or lifestyle (environmental or social networks), or a combination of the above. Taking medication long term is a serious decision for any person. Without understanding the systemic problems creating the symptom or understanding the balance between benefit and risk, smart decision making is impossible.

From a business perspective, one can see quick fixes all the time. For example, consider companies that make parts for various products, such as computers or cell phones. Suppose the production of a chip or a sim card falls behind. In that case, Company A is responsible for the lag in Company B, resulting in delays, lost business, and sometimes elevated prices. A quick fix would be to divert resources from all other productions to speed up the component in danger of being delayed; yet, that steamrolls into other orders and creates the same cascading effect. Systems thinking, instead, would encourage Company A to figure out why production is falling behind schedule: is it equipment related? Worker-related? Conceptually flawed (unrealistic expectations)? The temptation for the quick fix is undoubtedly linked to the fear of losing profit, even losing solvency, but in these scenarios, the quick fix can often fail long term and result in the same failures.

From an organizational (non-profit) perspective, quick fixes often have to be pressed into service because the time and expense are unavailable for the long-term solution. For example, to fully confront the AIDS crisis in Africa, one would have to assemble the resources for better education and a widespread push to reform underlying social systems that discourage prophylactic use and leave marginalized groups without much voice (women, primarily, in this instance). The quick fix is to get medications out to as many people as resources (and attitudes) allow, which does nothing to combat the fundamental problem. This is also the case with global crises wherein internal conflict prevents long-term thinking or external intervention. When a civil war creates famine (such as in Yemen), the only humanitarian response must be the urgent one: to get food to as many people as possible as quickly as one can. Yet, this does not address the crisis's fundamental causes: the collapse of political and economic systems that undergird the conflict.

Typically, fixing the systemic issue rather than addressing the surface symptom requires a two-pronged approach: first, you must shift your mental model into recognizing that the sign is not the problem, and second, you must be agile enough to take action with immediacy and urgency; get to the underlying issues sooner rather than later. If you have a leaky roof and run around every time it rains, putting buckets under the leaks, and you're indeed not fostering a real solution. Even if you patch up the leaky spots, it stands to reason that more will arise: what's causing the leaks?

The most significant danger in utilizing the quick fix is that its further damages or impedes the system's productivity. Being medicated for a symptom does not address the underlying systemic problem. If you are presenting with hypertension because you live in an abusively stressful situation, then no medication amount in the world will improve your health. The potential side effects of taking the drug, in this case, may very well outweigh the potential benefits. Besides, your health outcomes won't measurably improve if your environment is so toxic that it is damaging the balance of your biological system. This is why tackling such big pictures issues like addiction and abuse can be so challenging: the problem with the serial addict or abuser isn't the drinking or the inappropriate expression of anger—these are the symptoms—but rather the underlying systemic damage that needs attention and repair (psychological, environmental, social, chemical). This is why incarceration is an incredibly ineffective way to deal with addiction, especially: surface punishment does not alleviate the underlying problems within the person that leads them to this socially and personally destructive behavior, and so many returns to old patterns of action as soon as they are released. This method of dealing with the problem indicates a traditional, top-down approach, wherein one authority decides for an individual and metes out punishment from above. In the systems thinking approach, the addict-criminal would be treated for the underlying causes of the symptom and be an active participant in their treatment. As we enter a new era wherein there is a national call for a reevaluation of our systems of incarceration while at the same time there is an undeniable national crisis regarding opioid addictions, the quick fix solution is revealed for the patchwork of ineffectiveness that it has been for years.

Chapter 31: How to Improve Your Thoughtful?

Most of it lies dormant within us, or it is underdeveloped. Any development in thinking cannot take place if there is no mindful commitment to learning. You cannot improve your game in basketball if you don't put in some effort to do so, and the same is true for critical thinking. Like any other skill, the effort is essential for its development. As long as you take your thinking for granted, there is no way in which you can unlock your true potential. Development in your thinking process is gradual, and there are several plateaus of learning that you will have to overcome, and hard work is a precondition for all of this. You cannot become an excellent thinker by just wanting to become one. You will have to make an aware decision to change certain habits, which will take some time. So, be patient and don't expect any change to occur overnight.

Stage 1: You are still unaware of the significant problems or pitfalls in your thinking. You aren't a reflective thinker. Most of us are stuck in this stage.

Stage2: You start developing awareness of the problems in your thinking.

Stage 3: You try working on your thought processes, but not regularly.

Stage 4: You realize the need for regular practice.

Stage 5: You start noticing a change in the way you think.

Stage 6: You develop the ability to become insightful in your thinking.

You can progress through these stages by accepting the fact that there are specific problems in the way you think, and you start putting in conscious effort to improve yourself.

Making Use of "Wasted" Time

All human beings tend to waste time. That is, we fail to make productive use of all the time we have at our disposal. Sometimes we flit from one form of diversion to another without actually enjoying any of them. At times we get irritated about matters that are clearly beyond our control. At times, we don't plan well, which causes a butterfly effect of negative consequences that could all have been easily avoided by simple planning. Apart from all the time that we waste doing nothing, we start worrying about unnecessary things. Sometimes we regret how we functioned in the past, or we just end up daydreaming about "what could have been" and "what can be" instead of putting in some effort to achieve results. You need to know that there is no way you can get all the lost time back again. Instead, try focusing on all the time that you have at your disposal now. One way you can develop the habit of critical thinking is to use the time that would have normally been "wasted." Instead of outlay an hour in front of the TV flipping through channels and getting bored, you can make use of this time or at least a part of it for reflecting on the day you had, the tasks you accomplished, and all that you need to achieve. Spend this time to contemplate your productivity. Here are a questions that you can ask yourself:

When did I do my worst and best thinking today? What was it that I was thinking about all day long? Did I manage to come to a logical conclusion, or was it all in vain? Did I indulge in any negative thinking? Did the negative thoughts just create a lot of unnecessary frustration? If I could repeat this day all over again, what would I change? Did I do something that will help me in achieving my goals? Did I accomplish anything worth remembering?

Spend some time answering these questions and record your observations. Over some time, you will notice that you have a specific pattern of thinking.

Internalizing Intellectual Standards

Every week select any one of these standards and try to increase your awareness of the same. For instance, you can focus on clarity for a week, then shift towards precision, and so on. If you can focus on clarity, observe how you communicate with others, and see for yourself if you are clear or not. Also, notice when others aren't being clear in what they are saying. Whenever you are reading, see if you are clear about the content you have been reading. While expressing yourself orally or writing your thoughts down, check for yourself if there is some precision in what you are trying to convey. There are four simple things that you can make use of to test whether you have some clarity or not. You have to explicitly state what you are trying to say, elaborate on it, give examples for facilitating better understanding, and make use of analogies as well. So, you are supposed to state, then elaborate, illustrate, and lastly exemplify yourself.

Maintain an Intellectual Journal

Start maintaining an intellectual journal where you record specific information every week. Here is the raw format that you should follow. The first step is to list down the situation that was or is significant to you emotionally. It should be something that you care about, and you need to focus on one situation. After this, record your response to that situation. Try being as specific and accurate as you can. Once you have done this, your necessity to analyze your reaction and analyze what you have written. The final step is to assess what you have been through. Assess the implications - what have you learned about yourself?

Reshaping Your Character

Select intellectual trait-like perseverance, empathy, independence, courage, humility, and so on. Once you have selected a feature, try to focus on it for an entire month and cultivate it in yourself. If the trait you have opted for is humility, start noticing whenever you admit that you are wrong. Notice if you refuse to admit this, even if the evidence points out that you are wrong. Notice when you start becoming defensive when someone tries to point out your mistake or make corrections to your work. Observe when your arrogance prevents you from learning something new, whenever you notice yourself indulging in any form of negative behavior or thinking squash such thoughts. Start reshaping your character and start incorporating desirable behavioral traits while giving up on the negative ones. You are your worst enemy, and you can prevent your growth unknowingly. So, learn to let go of all things negative.

Dealing with Your Egocentrism

Human beings are inherently selfish. While thinking about something, we tend to favor ourselves before anyone else subconsciously. Yes, we are biased towards ourselves. You can notice your selfish behavior daily by thinking about the following questions:

What are the situations under which you would favor yourself? Whenever you feel egocentric, think about what a rational person would say or do in a similar situation and compare to what you are doing.

Redefining How You See Things

The world that we live in is social as well as private, and every situation is "defined." How a situation is defined determines how you feel and the way you act, and its implications. However, every situation can be described in multiple ways. This means that you have the power to make yourself happy and your life more fulfilling. This means that all those situations you attach to a negative meaning can be transformed into something favorable if you want it to. This strategy is about finding something positive in everything that you would have considered to be negative. Try to see the silver lining in every aspect of your life. It is all about perspectives and perceptions. If you think that something is positive, you will feel good about it, and if you think it's negative, you will naturally harbor negative feelings towards it.

Get in Touch with Your Emotions

Whenever you start feeling some negative emotion, ask yourself the following:

What line of thinking has led to this emotion? For instance, if you are angry, ask yourself, what were you thinking about that caused your anger? What are the further ways in which I can view this situation? Every situation seems different, depending on your perspective. A negative aspect makes everything seem dull and bleak and, on the other hand, a positive outlook does brighten things up. Whenever you feel a negative emotion creeping up, try to see some humor in it or rationalize it. Concentrate on the thought process that produced the negative emotion, and you can find a solution to your problem.

Analyzing the Influence of a Group on Your Life

Carefully observe the way your behavior is influenced by the group you are in. For instance, any group will have specific unwritten rules of conduct that all the members follow. There will be some form of conformity that will be enforced. Check for yourself how much this influences you and how it impacts you. Check if you are bowing too much to the pressure being exerted and doing something just because others expect it.

You don't have to start practicing all the steps at once. Start slowly and try following as many as you can. Primarily, you will need to put in a conscious effort for critical thinking to work and, over a period, these skills will come naturally to you.

Chapter 32:   Start Thinking

To start, let's look at how much you are thinking in general. Whether we are going to work, perhaps even at work, cleaning, hanging out with friends, or doing whatever else, you might find that you are only thinking for a portion of this time. When you are thinking, you might find that you have trouble sorting through your thoughts, or they are not relevant to the task.

In this Segment we'll talk about the wasted time you have in your schedule for mindless purposes. Some things do not require thinking. It is usually obvious which types of activities require thinking and which do not. If you spend time cleaning a stove, for example, you may have noticed that not much thinking is needed here. You identify what needs to be done (scrubbing the surfaces and using cleaning materials to clean the mess), and you do it.

Another example is walking the dog. The dog needs to get some exercise (so do you), so you take it outside, put on its leash, and walk for a bit. Not much thinking here. However, there are a couple of strategies to change this wasted time into valuable critical thinking time. One aspect of this is that when there is the context around these mindless tasks, it may be necessary to use critical thinking skills to make them easier or more efficient.

For example, you need to cook the pot roast at 1 PM, and it will take until 5 PM to complete the cooking process. Should you schedule the cleaning time before or after this process? This depends on a couple of factors; you will need to address your schedule for the day and think about how long it takes to clean the stove, and what the effect of cleaning the furnace will have on your physical and mental state, as well as coming up with a strategy to be an effective cleaner. The dog likes to be walked in the morning; if he is, he acts more relaxed throughout the day. You have a busy morning, so you must figure out a strategy to get the dog walked in the morning, as this is the optimal time to walk the dog while still addressing your needs and goals along the way.

Another strategy is to use scheduled thinking times for your mindless tasks. If you have a dog walk planned for 8 AM, for twenty minutes, find a way to incorporate some critical thinking into this time frame. For twenty minutes, you can sort through personal problems or things that have been holding you back. You can set yourself a schedule of thinking throughout the day that will compartmentalize your cognitive tasks.

This is easier said than done; we tend to slip into mindlessness. You must face this tendency and use intentionality to overcome it.

What does this mean? It involves at least some measure of self-talk. Self-talk is what you say to yourself in your mind. It isn't a verbally "talking" to oneself, but somewhat self-directed thoughts were characterizing our attitudes toward ourselves and our internal drives. Self-talk can go a little something like this: "I am starting to think about Betty at work. She is so annoying. Every day, when I go to get my coffee, it seems that she tries to get there before me so that she is assured a cup of coffee, even if I'm not." You want to shift this away from this type of thinking. Try to go down this route: "Betty usually arrives at the office at 9:30 AM. If I get to the office at nine and make my pot of coffee, I can avoid this problem altogether." Self-talk is necessary to route your mind away from the petty thoughts that it tends to gravitate toward and send you into a more productive headspace.

Self-talk is critical; it's a tool that will be very useful in solving problems and applying critical thinking skills. You can think of self-talk as one of the pillars of critical thinking. Each of us has "voices." This is not to say that we suffer from delusions or hallucinations, but rather that we have different ways of talking to ourselves in different moments. It can be helpful to identify and manage your self-talk by analyzing what you're saying to yourself. Some people have voices that tell them they are not right or that they have many negative attributes that they must focus on.

These voices may sound something like this: "You are no good. You can't do that. You've never done that before; you will mess up if you try."

This is the first layer of self-talk that you must defeat before developing your ability for critical thinking. If you have these types of voices that speak to you, try to talk back. Tell them, "I am good enough. I know how to try new things. If there is something that I want to do that is just out of reach, it is possible to overcome my challenges and reach what I need." This voice that speaks back to the initial self-talk should be gentle and reasonable. It should keep in mind the realistic expectations that are appropriate for the moment.

It might take some time to identify the various voices of self-talk included in your psyche; for some, they are challenging to disagree with. Some people have internalized these voices so much that they never question their self-talk. These kinds of people will have difficulty with critical thinking and problem-solving.

Being aware of oneself is an art and a science. Let's talk about both. Awareness can be art because, sometimes, the way that you can express what is going on with you can't be summarized in words. Sometimes, it is a feeling, an image, or a habit of thinking. Awareness of yourself may come in fleeting moments; you may be gazing upon a beautiful vista when you realize that your mind is uncontrolled to the degree that you desire, and that moment can be beautiful. Being aware of oneself can come through artistic pursuits, such as writing or making art or music.

These activities can help you become more aware of the cognitive processes in your life as well as emotional processes. You can sort out the moving from the cognitive and realize what needs to be shifted in your processing. There may be some tremendous emotional block to getting your mind into critical thinking. Where could this have come from? It may have come from an overbearing parent, who pressured you when problem-solving situations were nigh. It could've come from a particular experience or association you have with whatever situation you are facing. Connecting with nature, people, or art can help you make connections and become aware of when you are thinking and when you are not.

If we think about becoming aware of oneself as a science, we can think about how we can monitor our thinking. You may find it useful to write things down and keep lists. Many people like to write their thoughts out in different formats to become aware of what's going on in mind. You can keep count of how many negative views you have in 12 hours, for example.

This is a scientific formula-based way to do an "experiment" on yourself to gain insight. Here's a way you could format this experiment. For one week, without changing anything, record your negative thoughts. Every time you have one, make a mark on a piece of paper. Have the paper divided into one piece for each day of the week and try to specify when these negative thoughts arose during the week. At the finale of the week, you will have many data. Now comes the time to be a scientist. Go back through the week and try to describe what happened each day. Look for examples of times when you had excessive negative thoughts. You can find reasons and triggering situations in this method. Once you have identified the circumstances in which the negative thoughts arose, you can start to become aware of how your mind is working and what you need to do to eliminate those thoughts. For example, maybe you'll notice that when you wake up, the chronic pain in your foot makes you take a long-time eating breakfast. Then, your mind went into self-blame mode, thinking, "I am always late because of this stupid situation." You now have an objective perspective on this problem, and you can address your thinking appropriately.

Chapter 33: System Thinking Principles, Vocabulary, Tools, Archetypes

Systems thinking is a holistic approach to research that focuses on how the parts of a system interrelate with each other, and how systems work overtime and within larger orders. The path to systems thinking contrasts with traditional research, which examines structures by breaking them down into their elements. Systems analysis can be used in any research area and has been applied, among many others, to studying medical, environmental, political, cultural, human resources, and educational systems.

System action stems from the consequences of cycles of reinforcement and adjustment according to system thought. A strengthening process leads to an increase in some parts of the system. If a balancing mechanism does not search for reinforcement, it eventually leads to failure. An arrangement of balance is one that seeks to maintain equilibrium in a given system.

What are the forces that strike—the forces that cause these unintended consequences? Systems thinking provides us with a clue. Systems thinking is a method of looking at the world as one big system made up of many interconnected smaller systems. All of these parts can be linked via various positive, adverse, and nonlinear effects that can lead to unintended consequences.

The word "systems thinking" can mean different things for people. It is essential to note. The discipline of system thought is more than a set of instruments and methods – it is also a theory that underlies it. Many beginners like causal loop charts and control flight simulators are drawn to technologies in the expectation that these technologies will assist them in coping with persistent business problems. Structures thought, however, is also the sensitivity of the systemic existence of the environment in which we live; the understanding of the role of the process in creating the conditions we face; knowledge of the robust laws of structures which we do not understand.

Thinking technology is also a diagnostic tool. Like in the medical profession, accurate diagnosis accompanies successful treatment. In this sense, system thinking is a systematic method for a thorough and reliable analysis of issues before acting. This helps us to ask informed questions before we conclude.

Problems suitable for systems-oriented intervention have the following features:

Diagrams of Causal Chain. Recall, first, that less is more. Start small and simple; add additional elements to the story if needed—present part of the plot. The number of items in a loop will be dependent on the needs of the story and the individuals using the diagram.

A concise explanation may be sufficient to encourage conversation and provide a new way of seeing a problem. In other cases, you can need more loops to explain causal relationships.

Keep in mind that people always assume that a diagram will contain all possible variables in a story; this is not generally true. In other cases, external factors do not change very slowly or are irrelevant to the problem. You can complicate things unnecessarily by sharing this information, especially those with little or no control. Many of the most successful loops show links or interactions between parts of the organization or program that the community has not Forgoing identified.

Ultimately, don't ask if a loop is "right." Ask yourself then if the circle correctly represents the narrative the community wants to tell. Loops are brief explanations of what we consider to be a current reality; they are "correct" enough to represent that viewpoint.

The Archetypes

Keep it general and straightforward when using archetypes or classical stories in systems thought. If the community wants to know more about a model, then you can go into more specifics.

Do not attempt to "sell" archetypes; once people see the similarities between models and their problems for themselves, they will understand more. Nevertheless, you should seek to demystify the patterns by connecting them to shared interactions that we all share.

Change

Organization development experts report that change initiatives succeed only about a third of the time (and Lean implementation even less than that). By now you should know why: The people were not prepared.

I hope you also are thinking: People weren't prepared because the organization didn't create a safe, encouraging environment. Good, let's keep going.

As noted earlier, the change will occur if the current situation is unacceptable, and if a new outcome is highly attractive. After creating a supportive work culture, the next task in creating the right psychological environment is to give employees the sense that the current situation is not acceptable and that a new location will be better.

Be guided by two critical factors for successful change. One is a well-defined and emotionally engaging goal. The other is the meaningful involvement of those who will make the needed changes.

John Kotter wasn't the first with this concept, but he explains it well. The idea is that the need for change may be an intelligent assessment of the situation, but changing is an emotional experience. His book, The Heart of Change, is a classic.

William Bridges in Transitions: Making Sense of Life's Changes says that the emotional side of change is the "transition" from the known to the unknown, then to the new known. He postulates three stages: Endings, the Neutral Zone (which can be chaotic and New Beginnings.

A few of the concerns to note are:

Endings

· Am I acknowledging losses?

· Am I communicating enough?

· Do the employees have sufficient and accurate information?

· Are we measuring progress and defining the end (of the old)?

Neutral zone

· Are we accepting the reality of the neutral zone?

· Are we measuring progress?

· Are we safe from more attacks?

· Do people feel supported?

New beginnings

· How are people feeling?

· Are the new elements clear?

· Are we celebrating?

· Have we re-formed into our new teams?

Ignore the emotional elements of change at your peril. If you ignore the psychological aspects or don't know how to manage them, as my math professor used to say, "You may as well turn in your slide rule and check out a chorus robe." (A slide rule was an ancient mathematical computation device similar in appearance to a short, thick ruler, often worn in holsters by engineering students. They were replaced by handheld calculators, which, I believe, were also dressed in holsters by engineering students.)

Kotter notes eight steps to effective change at the organization level:

1. Increase urgency

2. Build the guiding team

3. Get the vision right

4. Communicate for buy-in

5. Empower action

6. Create short-term wins

7. Don't let up

8. Make change stick

In a nutshell, Kotter says, "We see, we feel, we change."

That's our target: To create an organization that supports people's emotional needs, to help them perceive what is critical, to encourage them to try new things to solve significant problems, and to work hard together

to eliminate process waste and improve value.

Chapter 34:   Why Systems Works

It is also a theory that underlies it. Many beginners like causal loop charts and control flight simulators are drawn to technologies in the expectation that these technologies will assist them in coping with persistent business problems. Structures thought, however, is also the sensitivity of the systemic existence of the environment in which we live; the understanding of the role of the process in creating the conditions we face; knowledge of the robust laws of structures which we do not understand.

Thinking technology is also a diagnostic tool. Like in the medical profession, accurate diagnosis accompanies successful treatment. In this sense, system thinking is a systematic method for a more thorough and reliable analysis of issues before acting. This helps us to ask informed questions before we conclude.

Systems analysis also requires shifting from events or data to behavioral overtime trends and processes underlying these trends and developments. We will extend the options available, and create more meaningful, long-term solutions for chronic issues by identifying and modifying systems that are not well served (including our mental models and perceptions).

Generally, the viewpoint of systems thinking requires curiosity, insight, compassion, preference, and courage. This approach requires the ability to look at the situation in more detail, realize that we interconnect, recognize that an issue often includes multiple solutions and championship approaches that might not be common.

The tools are capable vehicles to define, explain, and communicate your system's understanding, particularly in groups.

When Should We Use Systems Think?

The problem is relevant.

The problem is persistent, not one-off.

The issue is well known, and its history is well known.

People have tried to solve the problem unsuccessfully before.

Where Should We Start?

Once you start to tackle a question, avoid assigning blame (a commonplace for teams to begin a talk about!). Concentrate instead on topics that people tend to brush about and seek to raise awareness of the issue under consideration. To focus the conversation, ask, "Why are we not aware of this problem? "Stress the iceberg concept to get the whole story out. Let the group explain the problem in all three ways: incidents, trends, structures (see "The Iceberg").

Finally, we always presume that everybody has or knows the same knowledge about the past. Therefore, diverse viewpoints are necessary to ensure that all views are reflected and solutions adopted by those who choose to take them. You can be shocked to discover how different the mental models are from yours if a question is talk about by people from various departments or functional areas.

How Do We Use Systems Thinking Tools?

Diagrams of Causal Chain. Recall, first, that less is more. Start small and simple; add additional elements to the story if needed—present part of the plot. The number of features in a loop will be dependent on the needs of the story and the individuals using the diagram. A concise explanation may be sufficient to encourage conversation and provide a new way of seeing a problem. In other cases, you can need more loops to explain causal relationships.

Keep in mind also that people always assume that a diagram will contain all possible variables in a story; this is not generally true. In other cases, external factors do not change, change very slowly, or are irrelevant to the problem. You can complicate things unnecessarily by sharing this information, especially those that you have little or no control over. Many of the most successful loops show links or interactions between parts of the organization or program that the community has not Forgoing identified.

Ultimately, don't ask if a loop is "right." Ask yourself then if the circle correctly represents the narrative the community wants to tell. Loops are brief explanations of what we consider to be a current reality; they are "correct" enough if they represent that viewpoint.

How Do We Know That We've "Got It"?

Here is how you can tell you that you have had a handle on systems thinking:

You ask different types of questions, then you have Forgoing requested.

You hear "catchphrases" raising flags of caution. For example, if anyone says: "We need more (sales, revenue), the question is that we need more."

You start noticing archetypes and balancing and reinforcing processes in stories you hear or read.

You're looking at visual models (both your own and others' versions).

You know the leverage points for classic stories about structures.

You may want to move towards more complicated models of system accumulator and flow diagrams, flight simulators, or simulation software when you have started using devices that are designed for investigations and diagnostic purposes. Nevertheless, cognitive processes will also change the way you think about the environment and solve problems.

Here are four basic systems principles that will give you an understanding of what systems are doing.

The boundary of systems and environment: To consider the many entities and processes in the world as systems, we need to mark a barrier between the system concerned and its environment. If we want to see a family as a network, for example, we could separate family members from the schools, neighborhoods, and places where they regularly participate. When we were to see a cell as a system, the cell wall may be the boundary. Remember that when viewed from another angle, the device environment may be other systems. Limitations of systems-environment can be physical or mental.

Open versus closed systems: specific systems are relatively closed, which reduces the impact their environments have on their operations to a minimum. In contrast, more open systems can change significantly, depending on their environment's inputs. For instance, a small company is far more a free system than a car engine: the company is always developing and changing to survive, while the driver must remain the same.

Self-contained: One feature of the systems is that the systems comprise all processes and components needed for their different functions. Of course, nearly all systems take some environmental inputs (or other methods) and transform them into outputs. However, healthy systems can perform their functions self-contained (based on ecological data and return to the environment).

Adaptive: Some systems with greater complexity, such as biological and social systems, can adapt to changing environmental conditions. In other words, they can often adapt and survive. They even prosper, even if the environment changes over time (i.e., macro-weather patterns, types of food, changes in other social systems, etc.).

Chapter 35:   System Traps and Opportunities

Instead of taking the microcosmic view, systems thinking, ask each stakeholder to make the macrocosmic view. You are not merely an actor participating in the order; you are a stakeholder in the very design and function of the system itself. One of the key concepts within systems thinking is that we are not merely the operators of the systems but also the actual designers. Therefore, we must work to understand better how systems behave and how we can apply that knowledge to more functional designs.

We don't necessarily create systems consciously, particularly the amorphous systems of social constructs or cultural ideals. But, when we begin to understand the underpinnings of these systems, we can consciously address the fundamental problems that arise within them. Eventually, we learn how to move from the superficial level of diagnosing problems that occur within the system to understanding how to change the policy itself.

Within systems, thinking is an emerging branch of systemic design, wherein one moves from acting within a system—or multiple systems—to understand how to design a system. The systemic design does not apply to all challenges we face today—some problems are too changeable and too complex to layout a particular design. Nevertheless, understanding some of the critical components to systemic design can help us to grapple with the particulars of specific areas, especially if there are multiple stakeholders with different goals.

First, there is a base framework that systemic design follows, starting with the assumption that events and micro-systems are perpetually changing, which makes them fundamentally unpredictable. Therefore, any kind of system design must be inherently flexible and provisional, responsive to redesign when necessary. Social systems undergird any systemic design project that is undertaken; no purely corporate or political system exists without the complicating factors of social expectations and cultural norms (also in flux). However, social networks and the patterns derived from them are socially constructed; that is, they can be reconstructed. For example, specific social systems that prevented women from entering and prospering in the workplace persist today, though many of those attitudes have been renovated over time and through political effort. Last, small and incremental efforts are what drive systemic design. Sudden and sweeping change is not the goal, as it usually does not promote a sustainable outcome.

There are three levels in systemic design thinking, all of which are mutually reinforcing. First of all is a mindset, or what we might also call mental models, which determine how we approach the project at hand. The values within the mindset are a set of desirable characteristics that influence individual participant actions, such as organizational skills, evaluative precision, and explanatory communication. The mentality of a systemic designer should be able to interpret events and systems to inform the implementation of methods. The mindset should also express habits of behavior that are both open to change and resistant to stagnation. For example, a mindset that is continuously questioning is an asset, probing various possibilities. Allowing oneself to change based on context and information is also crucial, as is the ability to work in cooperative environments.

The second key concept in systemic design thinking is the methodology, which is an abstract set of guidelines that assist in applying methods. That is, the methodology is a system in itself that is used in a particular area of interest. In systemic design, the methodology reflects all of the systems were thinking fundamentals that we have covered so far in this text: inquiring beyond the system, framing ideas, formulating processes, generating outcomes, facilitating cooperative work, and reflecting on feedback. This requires an understanding of the interdependence of systems themselves; the thinking beyond particular frameworks to create new collaborations; the facilitation of original ideas and strategies to allow novel ideas to emerge; the utilization of feedback loops in a non-linear fashion to respond to all stakeholders; the understanding that multiple causes can result in various outcomes; and the ability to map it coherently.

Finally, there is the method itself, which consists of the tools of the trade that we have talk about throughout the book, in each of the problem-solving piece in particular. Also, methods aid designers in visualizing and modeling the system so that problems can be identified as the system are created, and room for new ideas is made. When the system design is in place, the stakeholders must decide to adopt the system and adapt the system as it is implemented, always cognizant of the changeable nature of the sophisticated world. Then, stakeholders can expand the network, creating more room for growth or expansion, and respond to questions and problems as they arise.

Chapter 36:   Living in a World of Systems

Types of Systems

(1) Closed systems:

Theoretical systems that do not communicate with the world and are not affected by its surroundings. Only the components are essential inside the system. Example: a sealed container— nothing goes into or exits the jar, but anything inside can communicate.

(2) Open structures:

Real-world systems whose boundaries permit the exchange of resources, materials, and knowledge with the broader external environment or structure in which they reside

The definition of a system Science system thinkers considers that:

• Energy, material and information flow between the various elements that make up the system;

A holistic structure is any collection of interdependent or temporally interacting pieces (groups). Systems are usually systems themselves and consist of other networks, just as components are typically parts of other structures or colons.

Scientific systems and the application of experimental system analysis is divided into three categories based on the methods used to tackle

Hard system systems—

Including simulations, often using computers and research/management science process techniques. Suitable for problems that can be quantified justifiably. However, it cannot easily take unquantifiable factors (opinions, history, politics, etc.) into account, and can treat people as passive rather than nuanced motives.

• **Soft systems**

For systems that cannot be easily quantified, especially those involving people with multiple and contradictory reference frameworks. It is useful to consider motivations, points of view, and experiences and talk about both the qualitative and quantitative aspects of problem situations. Soft systems are an area that uses empirical foundation work developed by Peter Check land, Brian Wilson, and their associates at the University of Lancaster. Morphological analysis is a complementary method of structuring and evaluating complex problems that are not quantifiable.

• Evolutionary processes

Bela H. Baath has developed a technique applicable to the design of complex systems in society. This approach combines an analysis of critical systems with methodologies for flexible systems. Compared to dynamic systems, evolutionary systems are known as transparent, complex systems but with the capacity to evolve. Baath successfully combined the interdisciplinary viewpoints of study into processes (including disorder, uncertainty, and cybernetics), cultural anthropology, the theory of evolution, and others.

Systems Approach

Systems thought approach includes many principles:

• The interdependence of objects and their attributes —

Individual entities can never constitute a system

• Holism

A holistic approach should describe emerging properties that cannot be identified by analysis

• Goal search

Systemic interaction must result in some goal or final state

- Inputs and outputs

- Entropy

The amount of chaos or randomness present in any system

- Control

A feedback mechanism is required for the operation to function predictably

Achievement of the same goals

Some examples:

- Instead of attempting to improve a car's braking system by looking closely at the material composition of the brake pads (reductionist), the braking system scope may be expanded to include interactions between:

As a result of such research, new insights can be obtained into how the store operates, why it has issues, how it can be changed, or how the other components can be affected by changes made to one element.

The components in a structure are the most unaffected parts to understand because they are observable most of the time. So, people frequently work on those to boost device performance. But to understand their behavior, you have to observe a method. Yet the hardest part of a system sees its

work or purpose.

Chapter 37:   High Efficiency Problem Solving

While we like to believe in the foundational myth that "all men are created equal" and the subsequent "American dream" fable that suggests we all have equal opportunity, it is most often the case that, within systems, unconscious bias creeps in and those who are perceived as successful are granted more opportunities for success. Necessarily, what can happen in an order that is left unexamined is that structural forces are more responsible for an individual's success than talent or effort.

For example, take the pay disparity between male and female workers, a well-known and oft- talk about systemic problem within the American workforce. The reasons for this are amorphous and multi-faceted, but there are a few factors that most agree are responsible for this inequality. First, women are perceived as less committed to work and more committed to family. If a young woman doesn't even have children, she is often passed over for promotion out of a preconceived fear that, once she does have children (for it is her biological destiny—another socially derived bias), she will cost the organization time and money with maternity leave and fewer hours. Second, women are perceived as less aggressive, which hinders their prospects for both hiring and promotion, particularly in specific segments of the business world that reward bold behavior. Third, the elements of patriarchy are still firmly entrenched in our vision as to what the structure of a system should look like, with a male authority figure at the top; this unconscious social bias leads to a lack of opportunity for promotion and leadership, which itself, in turn, leads to fewer examples to inspire younger generations of women to aim for such roles. Thus, a man and a woman of equal talent and equal education do not have equal opportunity within most, if not all, organizations; and once workers reach middle age, the success of the male who has been promoted outstrips the female's earning power. Women who do decide to have children and take maternity leave—some drop out of the workforce for long periods— subsequently fall behind in the race to the top. This necessarily leads to an under-utilization of more than half the workforce.

This type of self-fulfilling prophecy can also happen quite accidentally, without ingrained social bias or traditional preconceptions. For example, the productivity of an individual or a team can be the result of the organization's structure. If two groups rely on the attention and resources of one manager and one budget, then without careful monitoring and oversight, it often happens that these resources are doled out unevenly. Thus, the team that receives more feedback from the manager achieves more successful goals and subsequently given more opportunities for more future success.

This happens within social systems, and we frequently express our displeasure in this inequality: the rich get richer, while the poor get poorer; "you have to have money to make money,"; and the system is designed to suppress economic mobility. It is no secret that children of wealthy families have more educational opportunities—not just better schools, but better extracurricular activities and exposure to the cultural trappings of wealth—thus more success later in life. This argument is not limited to success defined merely as wealth; it is also true that successful people who enjoy better financial prosperity also enjoy better health and more security. One of the primary goals of many philanthropic organizations is to level this playing field, but the problem has often been that there are surface fixes (scholarships, for example) rather than systemic changes (equal funding for school districts, for instance, as opposed to relying on property taxes and the like).

This archetype is a particularly pernicious one because it is often hard to see it when you are already trapped within it. One cannot know about (most) opportunities that were missed because of being passed over or offered a lesser chance. We become unwitting victims of this systemic imbalance and spend our efforts trying to be successful in whatever has worked for us in the past (reinforcing loop). One of the only ways out of this conundrum is for organizations to be pro-actively engaged with the structure of their system and how it consciously or not rewards the workers within it. The vision plan might suggest that the goal is to provide structural equality while negotiating with individual needs—that is, a woman is allowed to take maternity leave without fear of reprisal.

An overarching view of how to get out of this reinforcing loop is to create a different mental model for how an organization is supposed to work. If the goal is to create "winners" and "losers" (or, if not losers, then less successful contributors), then the system is inherently creating a competition that could be fraught with bias and self-fulfilling prophecy. Instead, in systems thinking, the organization should see itself as a healthy and whole organism, wherein each of the parts has an equal and valuable contribution to make. Instead of diverting resources to one successful group or creating too many workgroups to function well, invest time and money into developing supportive groups wherein everyone contributes equally, wherein everyone's time and talent are rewarded justly. This would require a radical overhaul of many American businesses wherein competition is valued over collaboration; collaborative efforts not only create a more level playing field, but they also lead to more innovative solutions to intransigent problems. If you have three separate design teams working on building the most efficient electric vehicle, wouldn't it be more successful to consider and cohere all of the ideas, rather than reward one particular team? To have "winners," we must create "losers," and in so doing, we suppress morale and foster resentment among the vast majority who cannot be declared "winners" in a biased competition. Instead, systems thinking suggests that we create "win-win" situations where everyone's unique contributions are considered and rewarded. The harder part is in addressing and changing the social systems that allow for entry into and promotion within the workforce in the first place.

Conclusion

Systems thinking is perhaps best defined as seeing possibilities in an ongoing, complex adaptive, physical systems. Within complex adaptive systems, individuals and organizations do not operate as isolated parts, but work together in dynamic ways to create change, challenge, or sustain the status quo. In our systems of modern industrialized society, these are complex adaptive systems.

Systems thinker conclude that there is a need for a shift in the very structure of society today. To change our approach to change, we must become aware of the genuine differences within our societies and organizations and their interconnections. Traditionally, we have been stuck with the practices of outdated tools such as the scientific and industrial revolution, which have not been designed to last. We have been led to believe that we can somehow escape from the consequences of limited resources, growing technologies and limited space, however now is the time to re-think our present and future generations. Our governing bodies, must be more inclusive of their people and in particular the younger generations.

As part of the rethinking we must have a shift in how we see ourselves. Right now our modern systems can only duplicate a version of itself outwards. In the future, we need to recreate more of the original in our ways, recognizing from within any particular part that the original system was a whole system with a life force. This requires us to understand the generation cycle of any system, from its birth to its death.

This is so that we better understand the life cycles of the systems we are trying to create to understand how to avoid better the boxes that we often find ourselves trapped in and how to create in new ways.

We have to take a broader view of the life cycle of all the systems we are part of. If we continue to be limited to thinking in terms of simple linear cause and effect chains, systems tend to behave in a way where one small change in a single place is destined to cause a change everywhere, for good or ill. Instead we must become aware of the more significant systems in which we live, and how these give rise to form and structure within all systems, and upon which we can act and react.

As a result, we understand that many different kinds of change can come from the organized or unorganized actions in a system. We know that we must look at the political structures these actions take place in and understand the economy, social structures, and other systems. This is only possible through systems thinking, where we take a fresh look at what it means to be human.

The person who has the most accurate model of reality and acts accordingly will win. Be that person, and beautiful things will happen to you shortly.

Taking charge of your life requires you first to take charge of your thoughts. This s because ideas are the basis on which our behavior and lifestyles are formed. Wrong thoughts lead to bad experiences and adverse outcomes, while good thoughts have the power to steer your life in a new positive direction.